A remarkable true story:
From stroke to critical, and praying for a miracle.

In the Blink of an Eye
AND

CW00953084

Sue Bloomfield

Seven Colour
PRESS

Published by Seven Colour Press

Paperback: 978-1-0685229-0-1
Hardback: 978-1-0685229-2-5
eBook: 978-1-0685229-1-8

This book is dedicated to 'Team Bob'

Team Bob consists of so many members who all played a vital and pivotal role in Bob's journey. I would like to thank everyone for giving their permission to be included in this book and for being an important part of this inspirational and miraculous true story. Thanks to Anne Marie and John (Bob's Dad) for proofreading these pages and to everyone who has helped in some way with the making and publication of this book.

Thank you everyone for all your love, support, care, and dedication shown to Bob, myself, and my family, through what was a very traumatic and difficult time!

Thank You x

Table of Contents

Introduction

A true and inspirational story, this book takes you on Bob's incredible journey.

When Bob collapses at work with a suspected stroke, it is expected that he will make a full recovery. However, when Bob's condition rapidly deteriorates, Sue finds her husband's life is held in the balance. As his condition escalates to critical, Sue, her family, friends, and the medical teams all find themselves fighting for his survival.

This heartfelt book holds deep, emotional, and first-hand experiences, including many messages and dialogue between Bob's family, friends, and the medical teams. With so many twists and turns along the way, Bob's all-inspiring journey portrays incredible endurance, faith, loyalty, hope and love by all for one man's fight to live.

To anyone affected by a stroke, their family, friends, and medical teams, I hope this real-life true story gives you hope and encouragement to never give up.

'Believe in Miracles'

A True and
Inspirational Story

PART I
From a Stroke to Critical

Chapter One:

Blue Lights and Sirens

I recall it well: Remembrance Day, Monday November 11th, 2019. It was a sunny but chilly November morning. I could feel the warmth of the winter sun as it shone through the window of the bungalow. Its rays illuminated a vase that was placed on the table, creating a vibrant rainbow effect in the open plan room. I did not know it at the time but, within the blink of an eye, how our lives would change.

While looking at the colourful reflection I was reminded of the many beautiful rainbows that had often appeared in the sky in days gone by, especially at particularly important and significant moments throughout my life. For me, rainbows are - and always have been - a great sign of hope.

As I continued to gaze at the rainbow reflection I found myself drifting off into the depths of my memory. I began reminiscing about the time we were waiting to see if our offer had been accepted on this very bungalow. It was our second attempt because someone had previously pipped us at the post. However, we had learnt that their chain had fallen through, which meant we had another chance to buy it. I can recall waiting in anticipation for news to see if our second offer had been accepted. As I looked out of the window of our family home, curiously wondering if we had been successful this time, there it was, a beautiful rainbow appeared high in the sky and then half an hour later, my husband Bob called to say that our offer had been accepted!

Everything went quite smoothly with the purchase of the bungalow and, in May 2018, we moved in. I remember how excited I felt on that day: the garden looked so picturesque with the spring flowers beginning to bud and bloom as the birds sang in unison with such sweet melody...... 'Yep, this is home!'

With a sudden bang, I found myself withdrawing from a daydream state. The noise of a parcel being posted through our letterbox had made the dogs bark. By this time, the sun had moved its position in the early morning sky and the colourful reflection within the room had now disappeared.

Bob was busy getting ready for work and I was waiting for our daughter Emma to arrive as she was coming to do my hair. Bob pinned his remembrance poppy onto his jacket, took the last sip of his tea, placed the empty cup on the draining board and gathered his things.

"See you later," he said as he patted the dogs on his way out.

"Ok," I replied and with that I heard the front door close and his car drive away.

The dogs looked at me with that eager stare thinking it was their turn to go out next.

"Not now," I said, "I'll walk you later."

Archie is a golden retriever. He was six years old at the time. And Honey a lab/retriever cross; she was three years old. They are very loving and, although different in their own way, they both have a lovely nature. Archie became part of our family when he was one year old, Honey joined us when she was fifteen weeks. They are both rescue dogs; I do wonder sometimes who rescued who!

With both the dogs still watching me, I filled the kettle with water, made myself a quick cup of coffee and sat down on the breakfast bar stool. Suddenly, the dogs started barking with excitement, which was a clear indication Emma was at the door.

'Great,' I thought, as I was looking forward to having my hair done.

We were both excited to catch up and were chatting about her upcoming wedding to Will.

"Only six months to go now," she said.

I told her Bob had already written his father of the bride speech, but there would be no peeking as he'd already informed me that it was safely password protected on his computer. We both laughed as Emma unpacked the hairdressing products. We continued to catch up with the rest of the family news, particularly about Bob's parents, Daphne and John. Only just at the weekend while out walking, Daphne had stumbled, fallen over, and broken her arm, but luckily John was with her at the time and able to call for help. I explained to Emma it would be very painful and her nana would need to rest. Bob had also said to me earlier his mum would be unable to play golf for a while. Daphne and John didn't live far from us; it was only a five-minute drive to their house.

"Your nana will find it difficult to cook now," I said.

Emma replied, "So that means Grandad will have to help with the meals, then."

We both laughed, knowing full well John couldn't cook!

I said, "I'm sure between me and your dad we can help out too."

Just then my phone started ringing and the phone screen indicated it was Bob calling, or so I thought. I answered, expecting to hear his voice but instead it was Rob, one of Bob's colleagues. He informed me Bob had collapsed at work and they were waiting for an ambulance to arrive. I put the phone on loudspeaker, so Emma could hear the rest of the conversation rather than me having to repeat things later.

I was concerned at the news of Bob's collapse as although Bob did suffer quite often from chronic fatigue, he was otherwise fit and healthy. This had happened so suddenly and unexpectedly. I told Rob to let Bob know we were going to come into the office and were leaving immediately, we would be there within fifteen to twenty minutes.

"Come on Emma, I'll drive."

Emma and I made our way to Bob's workplace and arrived just before the ambulance crew. As we went into the office, we saw Bob was sitting on the floor. He felt dizzy and unable to move his left side: he said his left arm and leg felt heavy.

Just then the ambulance crew arrived and asked what had happened. Bob explained that he had been sitting in his chair when his leg started shaking uncontrollably. He knew something was wrong and called for help. Pat the receptionist was on holiday at the time so Tanya, who was covering, heard Bob's call and came straight in to see what was wrong. Ironically, Bob was the company's first aider and instructed her on what to do. Tanya remained calm as she helped Bob onto the floor and then called 999.

The paramedics proceeded to assess Bob and informed us he needed to go to the hospital for further investigation. They lifted Bob onto a trolley and placed him into the ambulance and said Emma and I could go in the ambulance with him if we wanted to. We both discussed the options and Emma said she was happy to go with her dad and I would follow in my car.

This made sense as Emma wasn't insured to drive my car and it would be useful to have my car at the hospital, making it easier to get back home later. Bob had also driven his car to work that morning, so I arranged with Rob for it to be taken back to our house at some point. As the company insured the car this meant anyone could drive it and I knew it wouldn't be a problem.

With Bob all settled, the medics invited Emma into the ambulance and I waited in my car as the crew prepared to leave. Deep in thought, I wondered what could be wrong with Bob. The silence was broken by a notification on my phone as I received a text from Emma!

Emma: *Mum, I think I heard them say they are blue lighting him. Is that bad? X*

Sue: *Ok, well, that's good, at least they are getting him to the hospital quickly, are you and Dad ok, or would you like me to come with you in the ambulance now? X*

Emma: *No, we are ok, Dad said you drive, we will see you there. X*

Sue: *Ok, I will follow you in my car but I'm sure you will arrive first, plus I have to park, so text me when you get there and I'll phone you when I arrive so you can let me know where to find you. X*

Emma: *Ok x*

With the ambulance engine now running and lights on, they were ready to go. I followed behind, but it wasn't long before the blue lights and sirens faded into the distance as the ambulance raced through the traffic towards the hospital.

After arriving at A & E, Bob was allocated a bay. Although Emma and I were worried, we tried to make it light-hearted and joked with Bob.

I said, "It's a good job Emma hadn't already started putting the dye and foils in my hair, as I would have looked like a right scarecrow!"

We all laughed.

In that moment, the curtains to the cubical were pulled back and we could see the doctor. He entered the cubical area, pulling the curtains closed behind him. He introduced himself and started to explain that Bob's symptoms indicated a suspected stroke and he would arrange for initial tests and a CT scan to either clarify or rule out his suspicions. These tests were completed quite quickly, and the results showed a minor stroke in the cerebellum area of the brain had in fact occurred. The cause was due to a tear of the inner lining of an artery in Bob's neck, which supplies blood to the brain. The tear had caused the blood supply to clot, which in turn caused a stroke. (Medical Term: Vertebral Artery Dissection 'VAD').

Bob was admitted to the Stroke Unit and was placed in the Hyperacute Ward, he was given medication to treat his condition and was expected to make a full recovery. The Stroke Unit consisted of three zones: Hyperacute, Acute One and Acute Two. New patients were first admitted to the Hyperacute zone and checked throughout their stay. Patients would move through the different zones as they improved. Once in Acute Two, you could then expect to be discharged and go home.

Once Bob was settled on the ward, we informed our family, friends, and colleagues that Bob was ok, but would stay on the unit for a few days to be monitored and was expected to be back home within the week.

Bob was only fifty-four, a kind, loving family man and the best husband, dad, son, and friend you could ever wish for. He worked as an accountant for a local building company and was well respected there by everyone and considered a true gentleman. He was also a keen golfer and kept himself fit and active. Although he suffered from fatigue at times, his blood pressure and cholesterol had always been within a healthy range, so everyone was surprised and shocked the stroke had occurred in the first place! It's fair to say we were all delighted he was on the mend.

On my visits to see Bob at Colchester Hospital over the next couple of days, I also had the pleasure of meeting the Specialty Stroke Doctor, Dr El-rekaby. I would often be there when he did his ward round and checks on Bob. I could tell he was a very kind and caring man. He was very approachable and would always take the time to listen and explain things to reassure us.

It had been a few days since Bob's stroke had occurred and all appeared well, Bob was improving and Dr El-rekaby was happy with Bob's progress and explained they would be moving Bob out of the Hyperacute area to the Acute One zone.

"Before I go," he said, "do you have any questions?"

"Just one thing" I said. "Bob has mentioned that he has been experiencing a few headaches and I just wondered whether that is normal after a stoke?"

The doctor replied, "Sometimes stroke patients do get headaches, but we will monitor him and see how it goes but all obs seem fine."

"Ok, thank you" I said.

He then proceeded to leave the ward. I didn't think any more of it as Bob had been prone to the odd headache in the past.

It wasn't long before the tea lady arrived. She made Bob his usual cup of tea and gave him some biscuits. She was a very kind young lady and always cheerful. She managed the canteen on the Stroke Unit and was often seen on the wards bringing patients meals and drinks to their bedside. She would also help them to fill out their choice on the menu cards for the next day. It seemed Bob had made quite an impression on her, as she knew he wouldn't drink any other type of tea except Tetley!

As he dunked his biscuits into his tea, he started to tell me about the daily events on the ward: who was who and who was new. It made me chuckle. Bob continued to chat away, and we talked until the bell rang to indicate the visiting hours were over. I told him I would be back to see him tomorrow; we said goodbye, and I returned home.

As I pulled onto the driveway, I saw John, our next-door neighbour. I got out of the car and explained to him that Bob was currently in hospital after suffering a mild stroke.

John said, "Oh, I'm sorry to hear that. Give him my best wishes. If you need any help walking the dogs let me know." John and his wife Doreen were lovely neighbours, in the summer months, we had often shared a glass of wine or two over the fence although we hadn't known them that long!

We had only moved into our bungalow about seventeen months earlier after we had decided to sell the family home. Although it was a beautiful house and many happy memories were made there, it was too big for just the two of us once our children had moved out. At the time, we were still relatively young - in our early fifties – and, although Bob was reluctant to sell it, I convinced him that by doing so we would have more choice on finding a bungalow we liked and one that would provide a practical layout to suit our old age in later life.

With the move also came the time to review our pension and finances. At the time, we had sought advice from our trusted financial advisor, who also suggested we might consider giving each other power of attorney in both health and finance. This meant that if either of us were ever in a position of lost capacity, unable to express our own wishes or make decisions, then the other one could act on our spouse's behalf. It was certainly something to think about. In the end we decided to go ahead, so a legal document was drawn up via a solicitor and the courts and we decided to renew our wills at the same time. They certainly needed updating as our children were now adults and the guardianship instructions in them were no longer relevant.

The bungalow was almost perfect, the only major thing we changed was the shingle stones to a block paved driveway. Bob and I were truly settled and enjoying our dream home and it came with lovely neighbours too! As Bob was currently in hospital, I was grateful for John's offer to look after the dogs if needed; it meant that my visits to Bob could be for longer and I could spend more time with him.

As I approached the bungalow I said goodbye to John and thanked him again for his kind offer. Arriving at the front door, I could hear Honey and Archie barking. I let myself in and made a big fuss of them both. I then prepared my tea and gave the dogs their dinner and settled down for the evening. It wasn't long before Bob texted me from his hospital bed. He explained that he was being moved from Hyperacute to the Acute One Ward and I knew this was good news.

The next day, Friday 15th November, I pondered over whether to walk the dogs before visiting Bob at the hospital. I decided I would visit Bob first, as he would need fresh clothes for the day and a top up on toiletries. While packing his things, I also thought that, as he was new to the Acute One Ward, he would not know anyone, so I would go early to help him settle in. I gave the dogs a treat before I left, grabbed my keys, and drove to the hospital. Even though it was early, parking spaces were few and far between, but I managed to find one eventually.

I walked through the main entrance of the hospital and through the busy corridors towards the Stroke Unit. Once there I made my way to Acute One area; I could see an empty bed on the right where Bob should have been. A nurse informed me he was currently receiving help to shower and dress. I thought this was a little strange as the day before he had had the ability to do this without help. After about ten minutes, Bob emerged from the bathroom assisted by two members of staff. He appeared heavy and unstable on his feet. The nurses helped him back to his bed, but I could tell something was very wrong.

I greeted Bob, but he barely recognised me; his speech was very slurred, he seemed very drowsy, and was not as alert as he had been the day before. The nurses thought he was just tired, but Bob had only just moved to the Acute One Ward so the nurses there did not know him as well as the staff who had cared for him previously. I explained to them that Bob had deteriorated, and his symptoms appeared severe in contrast to when he was in the Hyperacute Ward. I asked them to contact the Speciality Stroke Doctor to reassess Bob. The nurses could see my concern. They were lovely and paged Dr El-rekaby straight away. Within a few minutes' Dr El-rekaby arrived on the ward and could see instantly that Bob had worsened.

Because of the unusually quick decline in Bob's condition, we discussed the possibility of another scan to see if there was further damage to the brain. Even though Bob's previous scan had been done less than 72 hours before and it was not normal practice to repeat scans before that time, because Bob had deteriorated so quickly Dr El-rekaby authorised another scan straight away. He also had other reasons why he felt this necessary, which I would come to learn and understand at a later date!

The next thing I recall was the porter arriving to take Bob for his CT scan. I remember walking beside Bob as he lay in the bed, the porter was quiet as he pushed Bob along the corridor towards the scanning department. I glanced at the paperwork and could see that it was marked urgent! Once we arrived, the porter knocked on the door and as it opened he handed over the paperwork. There were other people waiting but they took Bob in straight away. I wasn't allowed in, so I waited outside. I felt so numb as I was trying to digest what was happening. It was a while before Bob came out, but the porter was on hand to take him back to the ward.

As we got settled back into his bay, I wondered if I should contact my children and Bob's parents, but I felt it would be better to wait until I had the full facts and to see what the results of the scan would show, then I would have a clearer idea of what was happening. I decided to hold fire as I did not want to cause concern and worry for anyone, especially my children; as a parent you just want to protect your children, no matter how old they are!

The nurses continued to observe Bob, checking his blood pressure and oxygen levels etc., but I could see Bob had deteriorated even further. He was not responding at all, it was like he had switched off. The wait for the scan results seemed like an eternity. I could tell the nurses were concerned.

Bob's phone was beeping with well-wishing text messages from friends and family, who were responding to texts he had sent them the day before. Little did they know that at this point things had changed for the worse. As well as the beeps from his phone there were also the bleeps of the monitors on the ward. Then I heard a new noise: solid footsteps entering the ward.

As I glanced up, I saw Dr El-rekaby walking towards me and I could see from his facial expression the news was not good. He reached for a trolley on which was a portable computer which he wheeled across the shiny floor towards me and then proceeded to plug it into an electric socket near Bob's Bay. Once logged in, he began to show me Bob's latest CT scan results.

"I'm sorry it's not good news" he said. "Let me show you the two scans."

He explained that the first scan taken in A&E had showed minimal damage, a minor stroke to the cerebellum part of the brain which controls walking and balance and fine motor movements. I could see a small circular white shadow which was a different shade to the rest of the brain, but this was minor. The Speciality Stroke

Doctor then explained the image on the latest scan. I remember my heart sinking as I looked at the screen.

I could see the cerebellum but this time the shadow filled the whole area.

The scan showed an accumulation and build-up of fluid and swelling within the brain cavities. This was affecting the cerebellum with mass-effect, (Medical Term: Cytotoxic Oedema). Subsequently, it was causing an ongoing increased pressure within Bob's skull. He was in great danger of severe physical and intellectual impairment and even coma and death. His brain was continuing to swell, and his skull was now running out of room. I was told the whole area was affected and the swelling was centimetres away from affecting the brain stem. If the brain stem was affected, then it would all be over. Time was of the essence. Bob needed a lifesaving operation to relieve pressure on the brain or he would die.

My head was spinning, it felt like I was looking in on someone else, a bit like watching a film in slow motion. But as Dr El-rekaby continued to speak, I knew this was for real. The next words I heard him say really hit home.

"Unfortunately, we cannot do the operation here, it can only be done at two highly specialist hospitals. I need to contact them to see if either of them has the capacity to take Bob and check they can perform the emergency lifesaving operation. In the meantime, we will get Bob ready and make him stable to prepare him for urgent transport, this will be by ambulance and a specialist ambulance crew. We need to be ready to move quickly as time is everything, so he will be transferred with blue lights and sirens."

'This can't be happening,' I thought, it was so surreal. I stood there holding my head in my hands, all sorts of things were running through my mind. I remember wondering why they couldn't do the lifesaving operation there and, more worryingly, what if the hospitals that can perform the lifesaving operation couldn't take him?! I could feel a surge of panic building as all the emotions started to consume me. I felt so lost in that moment, not knowing which way to turn, but I knew I had to keep calm and not let the fear overtake me. I told myself 'STOP!' Then I felt a rush of adrenaline surge through my body; it was a race against time before his brain stem would become affected.

I tried to phone our three children. I knew Emma would be in the hair salon. Jim, our eldest son, is a primary school teacher and our other son, Mike, owned his own website company, so it is not always easy for them to answer the phone immediately. Nevertheless, I tried to call but I could not get through. I had no time to text all three children individually, so I phoned my sister Cheryl. I explained Bob's situation and asked her to phone my children and Bob's mum and dad.

I said, "Tell my children that they need to get to the hospital to see their dad as soon as possible. Cheryl, it is critical!"

Chapter Two:

Life Held in the Balance

As I was standing on the ward I could feel my heart pounding, I stood alone watching as the nurses and doctors congregated around Bob's bed. There was a real sense of urgency as they started to prepare Bob. The curtains to his cubicle were pulled across for privacy so the other patients on the ward could not see, but also so as not to cause them distress.

It was hard to watch my husband lying there and I was aware my children would be on their way, I wanted to make sure they could find me on the ward quickly but at the same time I didn't want to leave Bob. I decided to wait outside the ward entrance, so my children would be able to see me when they arrived. I could also see Bob's cubical from there and the many doctors and nurses who were going in and out as they prepared to place Bob in an induced coma. I was also aware that the other patients and visitors on Acute One were starting to realise that a medical emergency was now unfolding.

Suddenly I heard familiar voices calling from outside the corridor. "Mum! Mum!"

I recognised these voices instantly; it was my three children Jim, Mike, and Emma. I hugged each one so tightly. I was so pleased they were here as I wanted my children to have the opportunity to see their dad, just in case. At the back of my mind the fear was bubbling away: we had no way of knowing if any of the two specialist hospitals would have the capacity to accommodate Bob and even if they did, he would need to survive the journey first.

More familiar voices could be heard echoing in the corridor as my children's partners Lauren, Charlie, and Will, and my sister Cheryl arrived. We all stood in a big circle in the middle of the corridor just hugging and holding each other in disbelief at what was happening. As tears filled our eyes, all of us in that moment were oblivious to anything or anyone around us. Soon Bob's parents arrived too, followed by his sister, Julie, and brother-in-law Mitch. I explained to them what was happening. I watched as Bob's mum stood there cradling her arm in a sling. I could see that she looked in pain, I could also relate to the pain I saw in her eyes that day, as I was feeling the same type of pain in my heart for my children too.

All of us stood there just watching from a distance as the medical team worked on Bob. His consciousness was impaired, and he had now been intubated. A tube had been placed in his mouth and airways to help him breathe because he was not able to do this by himself. The team were collating medical notes and files in preparation, while Dr El-rekaby was in his office desperately trying to secure a place for Bob at one of the two hospitals. An ambulance crew had also been notified and placed on standby ready to go.

Suddenly fast paced footsteps could be heard outside the corridor as someone approached the ward, the sound of the these became louder and louder and then I heard a familiar voice say, "I've received a call from one of the hospitals, Queens can take him!" I looked up and saw Dr El-rekaby heading towards me, he seemed excited, but also relieved although there was still an essence of concern and urgency. He told me that Bob had been placed in an induced coma and was ready to leave for Queens Hospital in Romford. Bob would now be handed over to the ambulance crew who would be taking care of him. Once they arrived at the Neuro Critical Care, Bob would be handed over to the Neuro teams to undergo lifesaving brain surgery.

He continued, "I have asked that they keep us informed here at the Stroke Unit on how things go." He then handed me a piece of paper with the address of Queens Hospital and the details of the Neuro Critical Care department where they would be taking Bob. He explained that the family wouldn't be able to go with Bob in the ambulance, but we could meet Bob at the hospital.

Although Bob still remained in a critical condition, I felt a slight sense of relief. My eyes started to well up as I thanked Dr El-rekaby for all the care and support he had given to Bob and indeed, all the family. He replied, "Good luck!" and added, "I have a relative who had the same thing happen to her a few years ago, she survived against all the odds. Have faith!"

Just then, a lovely ambulance man introduced himself. He was of stocky build and had a kind and gentle face. He said he and his crew would be taking Bob to Queens Hospital and they were now going to transfer him to the ambulance. We could follow and see Bob before they left. Once Bob was in the ambulance, we all had an opportunity to see him and each in our own way told him to hang on in there.

Bob's parents went into the ambulance first, I could see the distress and disbelief on their faces as they emerged from the ambulance as the full reality of their son being in such a critical condition sank in. Once Julie and Mitch had seen Bob, John approached me and said that they would make their way to the hospital entrance near the car park and wait for us there. I went in next and stayed in the ambulance to support my children and their partners as they followed, two at a time, to see their dad. First Jim and Lauren, then Mike and Charlie, followed by Emma and Will. Cheryl then joined me. She told Bob in no uncertain terms that he'd better hang on in there.

As we both emerged from the ambulance door, my children and their partners were waiting for us. I observed the deep despair and sadness in my children's eyes, but this lioness wasn't about to give up on her cubs! Although my heart was breaking inside I knew I had to remain strong for Bob and my family. I told them that we were strong and that love always wins and we needed to remain positive.

We can do this, have faith, was the message.

The ambulance man gave me a big bear hug. "Don't worry" he said, "we will take great care of him and we'll see you there."

"Thank you" I replied.

As I turned to leave, he said, "Oh by the way…" I looked back at him, "I don't want you arriving before we do!"

I smiled at him and replied, "No, I won't. Like you, I also have precious cargo in my vehicle."

We all stood there and watched as the ambulance door closed and then made our way to the hospital car park to meet Daphne, John, Julie, and Mitch. By this time, it was dark and the ambulance was far ahead. Julie and Mitch stayed behind to arrange for my car to be driven home and I asked them to speak to my neighbour John and give him the spare key as he would look after the dogs for me.

With that all sorted and bearing in mind Daphne's broken arm, we all felt it would be better for her to return home as she was not in a position to make the journey and needed to rest her arm. John agreed to take her home and would remain there to look after her.

With three cars left, my children, their partners, myself, and my sister, all decided to travel together in convoy. We set the cars' satnavs for the Queens hospital destination, but I suddenly realised I would probably need the power of attorney document, so I asked Cheryl to make a slight detour to my house to collect it.

As Bob was now unable to make his own decisions, this is where the power of attorney would play its part. It would allow me to make decisions on Bob's behalf. I was aware that anyone treating Bob would need to see proof of the document and take a photocopy to keep for their records, so it was important I had it with me. I must admit, at the time Bob and I had set it up, I never thought in a million years it would ever need to be implemented.

Once I'd picked it up, we continued to make our way in convoy. I can't remember much of the journey to the hospital, I spent most of the time looking out of the passenger window wondering whether Bob would survive the journey.

Yet there were other parts of that trip so clear in my memory. I think we had Heart radio playing and I remember the roads were busy. I recall the lights on the cars and streetlamps were bright against the dark night sky as we drove to Queens that evening.

Arriving at the hospital car park, Cheryl lowered the car window and reached for the ticket from the machine. With the barrier now raised, we drove in. I remember the car park being somewhat unusual in its layout. We drove around, spiralling up through the levels as we navigated the different floors. The ceilings seemed quite low, and the parking bays were set out in different blocks. Although the car park seemed quite full, eventually we found some spaces and parked the cars. We soon spotted the lifts and stairs leading to the hospital entrance. We entered the lift and pressed the button for the ground floor level. The lift descended through the lower floors and then stopped, the door opened and straight away we saw a sign indicating the way to the main entrance. Pay machines for the car park were also situated on the ground floor, so we would need to keep our ticket safe.

As we walked into the hospital it appeared bright and well lit. There were an array of shops and cafes aligning each side of the main corridor and, unusually, I also saw a piano just inside the entrance to the left. To my right there was a beautifully decorated Christmas tree, it was very tall. The decorations on it were made up of many tributes and get well wishes, plus remembrance messages for loved ones lost. I remember thinking what a lovely idea this was.

A bit further in, to the left, there was a solid, partly curved stairway with side barriers of opaque glass which we found out was the start of the many corridors, stairs, and lifts which would eventually lead to the Neuro Critical Care Unit. As we reached the top of the stairs, I noticed there were distinct rooms associated with different faiths and religions, giving people an opportunity to go in and worship or pray according to their own beliefs. Continuing through the next corridor, I saw a sign showing the way to St Luke's Chapel. We carried on walking through each corridor following the route to Critical Care. I don't quite remember the rest of the walk or route; I suppose I was feeling a bit numb by this point and the shock of our ordeal was starting to set in, but I do remember getting to the correct department quite easily.

As we reached Neuro Critical Care, we saw the ambulance crew bringing in Bob from the other end of the corridor. I remember thinking 'thank God, he's survived the journey,' and then, like a synchronised dance, we met in the middle, at exactly the same time, right outside the double doors to Critical Care! 'What are the odds of that' I thought, especially as they had left well before us, and we had stuck to the speed limit!

The ambulance crew buzzed the door and were waiting for a response from the intercom, so we only had a few seconds to say hi to Bob. He was in an induced coma and we weren't sure if he could hear us, but we were told that it was possible, so we held his hand, told him we were here, and he was going to have an operation and how much we loved him.

Seconds later, a voice from the intercom asked for details from the ambulance crew and then they were immediately let in, but we were not allowed past this point. Instead, we were asked to wait and told that someone would be out in a few minutes to speak to us.

It wasn't long before a female member of staff came out to see us, she was wearing light green scrubs and carrying a folder. She took us to the waiting room where she clarified some details. I handed her a copy of the power of attorney document which she took, thanked me, and placed it inside the folder.

She was really lovely and spoke with a gentle voice. She informed us Bob had gone straight to theatre and was currently undergoing the operation. She continued to explain the procedure. "It is known as an EVD (External Ventricular Drain)," she said. "This is inserted to help drain the fluid and relieve the pressure on the brain. After surgery Bob will need to stay with us on Neuro Critical where we will care for and monitor him."

We were told the operation could take half an hour to an hour and informed that there were a few places where we could get a drink and something to eat within the hospital if we wished. We decided as there was not much more we could do, Bob was in the hands of the surgeons now, it might be best to get something to eat and drink and also to update Daphne and John on their son. The hospital had my number to call me if they needed me urgently and to update me on any news.

Although it was late, Daphne and John were waiting for our call and we updated them on Bob's condition. We said that Bob had arrived safely and had gone straight to theatre, but we managed to see him for a few seconds before he went through. They said they would come up to the hospital the next day but we understood it wouldn't be until late afternoon as Daphne also needed to return to her local hospital for checks on her arm. I said I would call with any news.

We followed the signs back to the main entrance of the hospital where the toilets, shops, restaurants, and cafes were situated. I remember passing the ground floor lifts this time, so it looked like we had come back a different way. A few of us took a toilet break before we all sat down in the coffee shop. Mike and Charlie sorted out the orders of drinks and snacks. Once purchased, they brought them back to the table for everyone. We took this time to text our closest friends to let them know Bob had survived the journey and was currently undergoing brain surgery (EVD drain). It was now a waiting game and we had no idea of how things would pan out over the course of the next few hours. Bob's life hung in the balance and again we were left wondering if he would survive. All we could do was wait and for me, most importantly pray!

Less than an hour had gone by and we knew Bob would still be in the theatre, so once we had finished our drinks we decided to pass the time by exploring the rest of the facilities. It would at least give us something to try and focus on and help us all to keep relatively calm, although there was certainly no doubt we were all thinking of Bob. It looked like the hospital was well equipped with a variety of places offering a wide choice of hot meals and snacks. Looking around, I saw quite a few doctors, nurses, and other hospital staff eating at restaurants and cafes. This was good to know; if Bob did pull through, this would be where we would be spending a lot of our time. There was also a newsagent which sold the usual items such as newspapers, books, soft drinks, bottles of water and sweets etc.

I remember how we all stuck together, none of us really venturing too far from each other. Now and again, I would see Cheryl and my children glance at their watches. I knew exactly what they were doing, because I'd been doing the same thing - checking to see how long Bob had been in surgery. It was a very anxious time for us all. My children were looking tired, so I gave them the choice to go home, but they wanted to stay with me as I knew they would.

It had been an hour since we had left the Neuro Critical Unit, so we decided to go back the same way past the lifts on the ground floor, as this seemed to be the easiest route. We walked back along the corridor following the signs to Critical Care and headed for the waiting room. We thought it would be the best place to receive news, whatever it may be. Once back, I pushed the button on the intercom and reception answered. I asked if there was any update on Bob. They said he wasn't back up yet, so I let them know that the Bloomfield family were back, and we would be in the waiting room ready for an update.

We all sat down mostly in silence just gathering our own thoughts. I could see a freshwater dispenser which I hadn't noticed before, so I took a cup and started to fill it. "Would anyone like some water" I asked, and with that those who wanted some followed my lead. I didn't think I was really that thirsty, it was more of a distraction technique. As I sat down, I took a sip from my cup anyway; surprisingly, the ice-cold water was well received.

While we were waiting, there was another medical emergency unfolding outside the Neuro Critical Unit. A young lad had been brought in by ambulance and, like Bob, he was also in a critical condition and was taken straight through to theatre. I could hear a woman crying and someone trying to comfort her. Soon other members of his family started to arrive and they began to gather in the same waiting room as us.

The waiting room wasn't that big, and some people started spilling out into the corridor. I heard them discussing what had happened to this young lad. I believe he'd been attacked and had suffered a major trauma to his head and was currently undergoing brain surgery. I could relate to their fear as they were also now waiting to see if their loved one would survive.

Eventually a nurse came into the waiting room and looked around, I assumed it was to see us. I was trying to gauge the look on her face to determine if it was good or bad news. The other family were also looking at the nurse to see if she had any information for them. She approached the women who had been crying earlier and beckoned her into the corridor and then lead her into another room adjacent to us. The rest of her family followed, and I also saw a police officer enter the room, once inside, the door was closed.

Suddenly I heard distraught voices and a mass of sobbing coming from behind it. I glanced around the room at my children, their partners, and my sister, we all looked at each other, kind of knowing what had happened. We felt so sorry for this young lad and his family; he didn't make it. This was also extremely hard for me and my family to witness and we were left wondering if this would also be our fate.

Time was passing, and the unit had become extremely busy with emergencies. I think it was around 9.30pm when a doctor eventually came in to see us. He informed us that Bob had survived the operation and was on his way back to Critical Care. He remained in an induced coma and would be monitored and observed closely for any signs of improvement in responses. It was quite late in the evening, but we were allowed to go in and see Bob for a couple of minutes. However, only two visitors to a patient were permitted on the unit. This was understandable, especially as patients on the high dependency intensive care unit were receiving critical care and visitors were asked to be mindful of that. It was also especially important to disinfect our hands using the hand gel dispensers and to roll up our sleeves to help prevent any chance of infection.

I went in to see Bob first and I asked Cheryl to come with me. As we walked through the double doors to the unit, we could see the nurses' station directly in front of us. To the left of the room there were two bays. Bob was laying on the bed in Bay One. He looked much the same as he had done when he was first blue lighted to Queens. The tubes and monitors were still connected to him as well as the life support machine and there was also the newly added tube/drain protruding from the top of his skull.

The nurse looking after Bob explained that with this now in place, it should help drain fluid to relieve the pressure. She said each patient had their own nurse, a one-to-one ratio, and she would be checking Bob closely, making notes and recording his progress. Over the next few hours or so they would expect to see some reduction in the swelling of the brain. I thanked her for all her care for Bob and said my children would be coming in next to see their dad.

As Cheryl and I left the unit, I had a quick chat with my children before they went in and explained to them what to expect. Jim, Mike, and Emma all took turns accompanied by their respective partners. Once everyone had been in to see Bob, we all thanked the nurses again and said we would be back tomorrow; however, I would also ring in the morning to check how he was before we left. I telephoned Bob's mum and dad to let them know he was ok, back from surgery and being monitored; they had been waiting for the call and naturally were very relieved the operation had gone well. I said I would call the hospital in the morning to find out how Bob was and would let them know. I also gave them the telephone number and said they were welcome to call Critical Care any time to check on their son.

'Thank God!' I thought. 'Phew!'

Bob had made it.

We were so relieved. There were happy tears, hugs, excitement, and an array of mixed emotions for us all. We decided it was now time to head home and get some sleep. This had been a very, very long and traumatic day. We made our way to the hospital car park, paid for the parking, and collected our exit tickets from the machine. We then discussed the plan for the next day. Without question, all of us would be back again tomorrow.

The kids had already decided they were coming back home with me and would stay the night so we all made our way back to Colchester. After arriving at the bungalow, I gave Cheryl a big hug and said I would call her if I had any news overnight, otherwise we would catch up tomorrow. We both hugged again.

"Thank you, Sis! Love you," I said.

"Love you too," she replied. I waved as she reversed off the driveway and then I went indoors. It was extremely late; the dogs were so excited to see us. I gave them both a big hug (much needed on my part).

"Would you like a treat?" I said. I reached into the hall cupboard and into the box of treats and gave them each a bonio. The kids sorted out the sleeping arrangements and prepared the spare rooms and beds, while I made us all drinks. John next door had left a note on the kitchen worktop. It said that Archie and Honey had been for a walk and had also been fed. They had spent most of the evening at his house cuddling on the sofa. 'How kind of John and Doreen,' I thought. I just couldn't believe how the day had panned out, I was so exhausted, it was time for bed.

Chapter Three:

Fighting to Survive

Understandably, none of us really slept that well. In between drifting in and out of sleep, I had spent most of the night checking my phone to make sure I hadn't missed any calls from the hospital; however, I had managed to get a little bit of sleep.

As I awoke, I naturally glanced at my phone once more. The screen was displaying the date and time: Saturday 16th November 8.56am.

I was relieved to see there were no missed calls. I put on my dressing gown, knocked on the kids' bedroom doors and told them I was about to call the hospital to see how their dad was. Everyone gathered in the kitchen as I made the telephone call to Neuro Critical Care to see how Bob had been. We hadn't heard anything, and, as they say, no news is good news. I placed the phone on loudspeaker as it was important that everyone could hear.

The nurse looking after Bob told us that he would remain in an induced coma for now, but he'd had a comfortable night. They would continue to monitor to see if the swelling was reducing and he was currently receiving regular pain relief. I asked if it would still be possible for the family to visit Bob that afternoon and was told it would be. I confirmed we would be up later to see him.

I immediately called Bob's mum and dad to let them know Bob had

had a comfortable night and explained he remained in an induced coma but that was expected. I told them that the nurse confirmed Bob was allowed visitors today. I said we were all going back later this afternoon to see him, and they were more than welcome to join us. No doubt they wanted to see their son as soon as possible. Naturally, they would also let Bob's sister know.

I explained to John and Daphne that the early morning visiting hours had already finished, however the afternoon visiting hours on the Neuro Critical Care were 2.00pm – 7.30pm. As patients were only allowed two visitors to a bedside, we decided it might be best to stagger our visiting times. So, I suggested that, as the children and I had already seen Bob late last night, maybe they would like to go at the start of visiting hours from 2.00pm and the rest of us would aim to arrive at the hospital about 3.00pm - 3.30pm, where we could meet them to catch up. It was already coming up to 10.30am by the time we had all got showered and dressed. As we wouldn't be at the hospital until after 3.00pm, we decided we would set ourselves up with a cooked breakfast/brunch. It was important to look after our own well-being, especially given the circumstances. It was also comforting to know Bob would not be on his own as his parents would be with him.

I fed the dogs and refreshed their water bowl while Jim, Lauren, Mike, Emma, and Will organised breakfast. Charlie said he would go to the shop as we needed more eggs. Soon the room began to fill with the aroma of sizzling bacon. I remember taking a photo of the children as they were cooking, saying we would show it to their dad when he woke up.

Charlie had returned with the eggs and, with the breakfast now cooked, we all sat down at the table to eat.

"Mmm, this is nice," I said. "I think I might walk the dogs after breakfast, anyone want to join me?"

"Yeah, we'll come," they all said.

"Good," I replied, "It will be nice to spend some time with the dogs while we can and to get out in the fresh air and clear our heads a bit."

After we had finished eating, we loaded the dishwasher and

cleared up the kitchen area. "Right," I said, "who wants to go for a walk?" As soon as the word walk was mentioned the dogs both sprang into action wagging their tails with excitement, they knew exactly what that word meant for sure! It was definitely time to put on our coats and shoes, as the dogs weren't going to wait! I clipped Archie and Honey's leads onto their collars and we all strolled over to the local playing field. We saw children playing their usual Saturday league football matches as their parents were cheering them on from the side lines.

"Jim, this reminds me of you and your dad, when he used to take you to your junior football games," I said.

"Yeah, I remember Dad bringing me here once to play an away match," he replied.

We had been out for just over an hour and the dogs were having a really good run. As we made our way back home through the woodland area we enjoyed taking in the scenery and the cool fresh air. It was quite comical to watch the squirrels scurry up the trees as fast as they could as Honey and Archie approached! I remember how we all giggled at that. Having had a couple of intense and traumatic days it helped to take our minds off of things for a short while. It was also lovely to see the usual winter robins as they fluttered from branch to branch. It reminded me of Bob's first few days at Colchester Hospital Stroke Unit. Whilst I was sitting in the family meeting room, a little robin would often appear on the decking just outside the window. For me, just like the rainbow, robins are also a comforting sign. I still have the photo I took of it that day!

Once back indoors, we made a cup of tea. I knew that John and Daphne would be at Queens hospital by now and indeed at Bob's bedside. With the drinks finished, it was time to get ourselves ready to leave for the hospital. It would take just under an hour to get there anyway. I decided I would take Bob's car; it seemed the perfect choice, as everyone was insured to drive it if needed. We gave the dogs a treat and grabbed our keys and phones in preparation for the car journey.

Whilst driving to the hospital I found myself becoming familiar with some of the roads and I wasn't relying so much on the sat nav to find the way anymore. Again, once arrived, we parked up in the spiral carpark then walked into the main hospital entrance and went straight to Neuro Critical Care.

As we walked along the busy corridor, we caught a glimpse of the back of Daphne and John heading towards the waiting room. Jim, Mike, and Emma all called out to them. "Nana, Grandad!" they both turned around and saw us all heading towards them. We gathered in the waiting room where Julie and Mitch were also seated. They had all been in to see Bob and said that, although still in a coma, he looked ok, considering. Daphne and John had just come out from Neuro Critical Care because the nurse was making Bob comfortable and changing his sheets. They told us they had been talking to Bob but didn't know if he could hear them, however the nurse had said he may be able to. "That's good" I said.

While the nurse was making Bob comfortable and cleaning the tubes and equipment, we took the opportunity to chat and catch up with everything. We all said how well Bob had done to get through this and Daphne and John said they would help in any way they could. They thanked me and their grandchildren for all we had already done for Bob. They said what a lovely family we were and that they were immensely proud of us all. This meant a great deal to me.

I said I was going to buzz reception to see if Bob was ready for us to go in to see him. Daphne, John, Julie, and Mitch were ready to go home so we said goodbye and arranged to catch up later. I walked back towards the double doors at Neuro Critical Care and buzzed the intercom to let them know we were here to see Bob. "He is ready for visitors now," came the reply. I asked the children if they wanted to go in first to see their dad, but they said I should see their dad first, then they would follow with their respective partners.

As I entered the unit, I applied the gel from the dispenser to sterilise my hands. I saw a couple of nurses seated behind the desk of the nurses' station. Bob was still in the same bay to the left. In the next bay was a lady, much the same as Bob, all wired up to machines and monitors. Like Bob, she was also laying there motionless.

The machines were beeping as her 1-1 nurse sat at the end of her bed monitoring and documenting everything on her chart. As I approached Bob's bed, his nurse greeted me.

"Are you Bob's wife?" he asked

"Yes, I'm Sue. My children are outside and waiting to come in next," I replied,

"Aww, it's nice to see he has visitors, it all helps," he said.

"Yes, his parents and sister were in earlier," I replied.

"Yes, they were, I was talking to them, it's really good for Bob to hear familiar voices, it all helps to stimulate the brain," he said.

"Am I able to hold his hand" I asked.

"Yes of course," he replied.

He wanted to know if Bob normally did a wet shave. I explained that he did sometimes, but he also used an electric shaver. He asked me to bring it in next time I visited. He said that I could also bring in Bob's own toiletry bag. He explained that sensory stimulation was important and that if Bob had a particular aftershave, I should also bring it in, as the scent would be familiar to him. I remember thinking what a lovely and caring young man this nurse was, I really liked him.

I asked how Bob was doing and he told me that there was currently no change in his condition; his vital signs hadn't become any worse, but they hadn't improved either. They were checking the fluid output from the EVD drain but the amount collected seemed to be a little less than expected. They were hoping Bob would have started to show signs of coming out of the coma by this point. His consultant had just been in to see him and had booked an MRI scan to be done that day; this would give them a clearer picture of what was going on inside his brain. He continued to explain that they hadn't yet seen the expected response signs. It was possible that Bob needed a little more time, however, they needed to check that the fluid and swelling were decreasing enough after the EVD procedure just to be on the safe side. I started to feel a little concerned that Bob had not shown the expected responses. I hoped the nurse was right and he just needed more time.

I knew the importance of talking to Bob, so I held his hand and began to speak. "Bob, our children cooked me a lovely breakfast this morning and then we all took the dogs for a walk over the field. We saw kids playing their football matches, it reminded me of how you use to take Jim to his junior football games." He just laid there motionless, as I continued to chat.

At that point his nurse was called to the nurses' station for a telephone call. When he returned, he informed me that a porter would be arriving soon to take Bob for his MRI scan and he would also be going with him. I was aware my children would be waiting to see their dad, so I didn't want to take up too much time. I told him they were coming in to see him next. I said goodbye and thanked the nurse. As I came out of the unit, I could see all the children standing right outside the door waiting for their turn to see their dad. 'Bless them,' I thought. I explained that they should talk to their dad and they could also hold his hand as he needed to know they were there.

"The porters are coming to collect your dad for his scan soon, but I don't know how long that will be," I said, "so maybe spend about five minutes per couple to start with, to give everyone a chance to see him, just in case the porter arrives."

"Yes, that's a good idea," they replied.

In turn, they each went in with their partners two at time. I was so pleased everyone had a chance to see Bob before he had to go for the scan. The nurse said we could sit in the waiting room if we wished and they would let us know when Bob was back. He also said it was possible the results would be back quite quickly. We decided to stay as we wanted to know the results and to make sure all was ok. By this time, the waiting room was quite empty, however, we soon filled it as we all took a seat. Some of us helped ourselves to water from the dispenser, offering a cup to others if they wanted it.

It had been about half an hour since Bob had gone for the scan. We were all discussing the fact it was good he was having the MRI. Obviously, we were hoping Bob would be back soon as we were all eager to see him again. We were also hoping the results would be back quickly and would show an improvement. Our discussions were interrupted as a man in blue scrubs entered the room.

"Mrs Bloomfield" he said.

"Yes, that's me."

"Hello, my name is Raghu Vindlacheruvu. I'm the surgeon from Neuro Critical Care. Are you all relatives of Bob?"

"Yes, these are my children and their partners," I said. All of us were looking at him with such desperation, hoping it would be good news, but I had seen that look before and sensed it was not!

The surgeon continued, "Bob has had the MRI scan and I need to talk to you about the results. I'm really sorry but the results are showing ongoing evidence of mass effect, which means the brain is still swelling. It is now millimetres away from the brainstem and close to affecting the spinal cord."

I just couldn't believe what I was hearing. We had all thought Bob would be ok after the EVD (drain), when he had done so well to survive the surgery. I could see the emotional impact this was having on my children. I felt so sorry for them and my heart was breaking inside, but, as their mum, I had to remain strong. I could feel my body tensing and my shoulders tightening, waiting for the surgeon to say his next words. In that split second of silence the surgeon continued, "Bob needs to go to theatre right now if he has any chance of surviving." I can remember thinking, 'Thank God they can still do something'!

He continued to explain that the operation was known as a Posterior Fossa Decompression (Craniectomy). It involved cutting the back of the head and neck to remove a 5cm piece of skull and attaching a skin graft to the brain membrane. This would create more space and hopefully relieve the building pressure, helping to avoid damage to the brain stem. Bob would need to be placed on his stomach for the operation which meant that his vital organs would be under increased pressure more so than in a normal operation. The operation usually takes around two to three hours.

"As you hold power of attorney, will you consent to the surgery?" he asked.

"I need some guidance," I said. "I know Bob wouldn't want to live a life where he had no quality, and where his mind or body was severely impaired. What is the survival rate for such an operation, and will he have the ability for his brain to repair or recover? Will it be enough for him to have a reasonable quality of life, if the operation is successful?"

The surgeon replied, "If someone has a chance of life I will do my best for that patient. I believe Bob has every chance if we move quickly but once the brainstem is affected, then no! At the moment the brainstem is still intact, and the brain has the ability to relearn. Bob is relatively young and it's possible that Bob could regain at least 80% capacity, however, as this type of stroke is very rare, we don't have enough data to say so for absolute certainty. As with any operation, there are risks. It's possible Bob may not pull through the surgery. In the event of this, we would try resuscitation or you can request a 'do not resuscitate' (DNR). I believe it is a big ask but, without the surgery, Bob will certainly die."

My heart was racing. I could hear the beat of it pounding so intensely as I felt my blood pressure rising. I didn't know what to do, there wasn't much time and I had to think quickly. I had to keep calm; I needed to keep a level head and make the right decision for both Bob and my children. The atmosphere was so tense. I wanted my children to know their views were important and they could be involved in helping me in any decision making, if they wanted to. Although the decision making was difficult, I asked the question, "I think we need to give your dad a chance to fight, do you?" There was a unanimous YES, all around.

I agreed that the surgeon could go ahead with the lifesaving brain surgery, however we decided that, if Bob was to die during the surgery, then we wanted them to just let him go in peace. I signed the consent form straight away and a DNR was added to his notes. He told us we were welcome to stay and wait and he would come and speak to us after the operation.

"Thank you" I said, as the surgeon swiftly left for theatre. I looked at my children, I felt so scared inside at what we as a family might be facing. Although we had no idea of what the outcome would be, either way, I wanted to be there for my husband and my children and they wanted to be there for me and their dad.

I took a deep breath as my thoughts moved to Bob's parents. 'How on earth am I going to break the news to Daphne and John?' I worried. It was an extremely difficult thing to have to do, especially over the phone. I gathered courage and dialled their number. John answered. With my voice wavering, I began to update him on everything. John said they would return to the hospital at once. Obviously, they were upset and very worried but agreed we needed to give Bob every chance.

I then called my sister Cheryl to update her and, without hesitation, she said she was coming up and was on her way. Our closest friends would also want to know how Bob was, so I asked Cheryl to contact them but to explain that as it was not currently visiting hours, we had been told at this point only family were permitted on the unit. It wasn't long before I started to receive heart-warming and well-wishing messages from everyone. After about an hour, Bob's mum and dad arrived back at the hospital. I gave them both a hug. Julie and Mitch were also with them and we sat down in the waiting room. Soon after, my sister Cheryl arrived with my brother-in-law, Rab. Rab was very practical and decided to take orders for any drinks and snacks. He wasn't sure if the restaurants and shops were still open, but he had spotted a few vending machines if needed.

Surprisingly, the Neuro Critical Care corridor seemed busy again as there were people buzzing the intercom to be let in. Doctors and nurses were coming and going as new emergencies were arriving at the unit and there were other members of staff passing through the corridor to the wards next door. It wasn't long before Rab had returned with some refreshments and a selection of chocolate bars and savoury snacks. The children and I sent messages to the rest of our friends and family with the update and said we would keep them all informed on Bob's condition. All of us had so many messages from family and friends enquiring about how Bob was and all sending their love, wishing him well. Many were praying for him to pull through.

It had been nearly three hours since Bob had gone to theatre and we still hadn't heard anything.

I decided to buzz Critical Care to ask if there was any news. I listened to the voice coming from the intercom as a nurse responded, explaining Bob was not back yet. I was told someone would be out to see us shortly and would meet us in the waiting room. I remember all of us were so worried and concerned for Bob but at the same time, we were trying to remain strong for each other, trying not to show how fearful we were feeling on the inside. After about fifteen minutes, a nurse came out to see us. She said Bob was still in theatre but she had spoken to the surgeon who said the operation was going to plan. All things being equal, afterwards Bob would return to Neuro Critical Care. There had been other emergencies admitted that night, so it was unlikely that the surgeon would be able to see us later. As it was late, we were advised to go home and get some rest. They would phone us as soon as Bob was back in Neuro Critical Care.

As we were leaving the hospital grounds, we all discussed tomorrow's plans before Julie and Mitch drove John and Daphne back home. Cheryl and Rab also returned home and everyone agreed to wait for me to call them once I'd heard from the hospital. They all said they didn't care how late it was, they still would like me to call or text with any news. My children and their partners were adamant that they would be coming back home with me and would stay over again. Mike and Charlie detoured to their home in Maldon to collect some toiletries and clean clothes, plus Mike's laptop so he could work from mine; he was planning to stay for a while as he wanted to be more local and on hand. Jim and Lauren arranged for their clothes and toiletries to be dropped off by Lauren's mum in the morning. Emma and Will also went home to collect their things and then everyone returned back home to mine.

It was a long night and none of us went to bed. There was no way any of us would be able to sleep anyhow. We were all waiting for the phone call and midnight was fast approaching. I wondered if I should wait a little longer for the hospital to call me as they promised they would, but not knowing was a terrible feeling. I wanted to call, but at the same time I felt so scared of what the news might be that I didn't want to call at all.

I took a deep breath, dialled the Neuro Critical Care number, and placed the phone on loudspeaker. The phone started ringing as the call connected. It took a few moments before a female voice answered.

"Hello, Neuro Critical Care, how can I help?"

"Oh, hi, its Sue, Bob Bloomfield's wife. Is there any news about Bob yet please?"

"One moment, let me check, please hold the line."

The silence that followed felt like an eternity. I silently prayed 'Please God please let Bob be ok.' Eventually I heard the phone click and a male voice spoke.

"Mrs Bloomfield?"

"Yes, speaking, my children are with me and are listening as well," I replied.

"That's ok. I'm the surgeon. I apologise for the delay making contact. Unfortunately, we've had lots of emergencies tonight, but I have just left the theatre, so I can speak with you." His tone seemed solemn; I was so fearful at what he might say next. The moment of being stuck in limbo not knowing if Bob had survived or not was dreadful! I wanted to ask, but then I didn't want to ask but I had to know.

"Has Bob died?" I said, and at that moment all of us were holding our breath.

"Bob's made it," he said. I took a deep breath in, then out. 'Thank God, he hasn't died,' I thought, and let out a big sigh of relief along with the rest of my family.

The surgeon continued, "Bob is still in a coma, but we will again watch him as we did before and wait for signs of any improvement. We will gradually reduce sedation and ventilation to see if Bob is able to support his own breathing. We're hoping this should spark a reaction to wake up from the coma and that Bob will have the ability to breathe unaided. You will be able to come up and visit him tomorrow, oh, well, it's actually today now, isn't it? We believe it's important to his recovery that he knows you are there; hearing you and familiar voices will help to stimulate his brain."

"Thank you so much! Thank you, thank you, thank you, thank you," I said. "We will certainly be up to see him later."

Although it was now the early hours of Sunday morning 17th November 2019, we made the calls and texted everyone who had asked us to, to let them know the good news. Many had been waiting up and at least now things looked brighter. The past few days had been very emotionally testing for us all. The highs and lows over the past few hours had certainly taken their toll and by this time we were all absolutely shattered. Before we all went to bed, we decided that whoever woke first could call the hospital to see how Bob was doing and send a text to the rest of us. That way if anyone were still sleeping, they could catch up on their rest and those who were awake would also have peace of mind.

It was going to be hard to get off to sleep with all the adrenalin built up but at least we knew Bob was ok.

Chapter Four:

Chance to Respond

As daybreak was fast approaching, I found myself gradually waking up from the night's sleep. I opened my eyes as I heard the ping of a text message notification on my phone. I could see the time had gone past 9.00am and there was a message from Jim.

Jim: 'I've called the hospital for an update on Dad, they said he is comfortable and stable but not responding yet x.

I started thinking it was good Bob was stable, but I was so hoping that he would wake up that day. I was aware most people respond within a few hours after the operation and Bob was taking a long time to show any signs of coming out of the coma.

My thoughts were interrupted as the dogs began to bark and then I heard Jim and Lauren invite someone in. I could hear the commotion in the hallway; the dogs were excited to see someone. It was Tracie, Lauren's mum. She was dropping off some clothes and other bits and pieces for them as previously planned.

I put on my dressing gown, came out of the bedroom, and walked into the kitchen area where they were standing. I was aware it would be difficult for anyone to know what to say in these situations, which was understandable. However, no words were needed. Tracie was lovely and immediately gave me a big hug (one of the best universal signs to show you care). Jim and Lauren thanked Tracie for bringing their things over. She told them to let her know if we needed any help with anything. They said goodbye and she left.

I knew it wouldn't be long before Bob's mum and dad would also be here, so it was time for me to have a quick shower and get dressed. John and Daphne had previously said they would pop over to see us sometime during the morning and it was only natural that they wanted to make sure we were all ok. I have to say, I feel lucky to have such lovely parents-in-law and grandparents to my children. Daphne and John have always been there to offer help and advice when asked, but have never been interfering.

I had just made a cup of tea and had sat down to drink it when the doorbell rang again. I went to the door. I expected to see Bob's mum and dad upon opening it but instead I was surprised to see a lady standing there with a beautiful bouquet. She gave me the flowers and I thanked her and took them inside.

The bouquet consisted of the many beautiful bright colours you see in a rainbow. 'Aww, how lovely' I thought. I reached for a vase from the cupboard, filled it with water, arranged the flowers and placed the greeting card amongst them. I then texted my friend to say thank you.

It wasn't long after that Bob's mum and dad arrived. We greeted each other with a hug and sat down in the lounge area. Will and Emma made the drinks for everyone and we began to update John and Daphne. Jim explained he had spoken to the nurse and was told his dad had had a comfortable night. They were expecting to see some signs of response by now and had concerns this hadn't happened yet but did say it was early days and everyone is different.

Obviously, all of us were going up to the hospital again that afternoon and a few of our closest friends had also said that they would like to visit Bob. As it was a Sunday, it meant they weren't at work. Although we knew people would always visit during the week, it was really the first time since Bob's stroke that our friends had an opportunity to see him. After spending some quality time with us, Daphne and John left to have their lunch and would be heading off to the hospital where we would see them later that afternoon.

It had been three days since my children had temporarily moved back in with me and we were working well as a team. As provisions were running low we all sat down to make a shopping list. This included the ingredients for the meals planned during the week ahead, something for our lunch, and new toiletries for Bob. As we weren't due to leave for the hospital until the afternoon, we had the whole morning to sort everything out before we had to set off.

Jim, Lauren, Emma, and Will said they would go to the supermarket to buy everything we needed, so I gave them my credit card to pay for the shopping. "It's on me," I said, as I didn't want them to worry about any extra bills. I also told them to take Bob's car which was fully insured so anyone could drive it. I also didn't want my children to use their own petrol or be out of pocket. Bob's car had a full tank of petrol anyway, so there was no point in it just sitting there on the driveway. It was a relatively new Mercedes and I thought it would be a novelty for the kids to drive it and a distraction from worrying about their dad. I gave Emma the keys and off they went. Emma's car was an old hand-me-down; needless to say, she was very keen to drive her dad's car.

Mike and Charlie said that they would sort out the household chores. With two big dogs running around, it was certainly time to get the hoover out. Understandably though, Bob's emergency had taken priority and we simply hadn't had time for the normal day-to-day things. With everything else covered, I decided to take the dogs out for a quick walk.

When everyone had returned to the bungalow, we unpacked all the shopping. I placed Bob's toiletries in a carrier bag along with his electric shaver and Hugo Boss aftershave and put it by the front door ready to go. After lunch we gathered our coats, I picked up the carrier bag and again we all travelled in convoy to Queen's Hospital.

Arriving at Critical Care, as normal we buzzed the door and visiting began as we took turns to see Bob. The waiting room became our central meeting and swap-over point. I went in to see Bob first to get an update from the nurse on any progress. As I approached his bay, I handed the bag of new toiletries to the nurse and she promptly placed the items in Bob's locker to the left of his bed. He looked quite comfortable as he lay there, with his eyes closed and the machines helping him to breathe. Due to the many tubes and monitors he was attached to and the surgery on his head, it was not possible for Bob to wear a T-shirt or top of any sort, instead a hospital gown was draped over him, and he was also covered with a sheet and the standard hospital blue blanket to keep him warm.

I leaned over to kiss Bob on the cheek; however, I couldn't help but notice a very unpleasant smell, it was coming from the area of the tubes in his mouth and airways. It was quite off-putting and I mentioned it to the nurse. She explained that Bob had a slight chest infection which is quite common for someone on a ventilator. She was certain this was causing the odour. She informed me that they are prescribing intravenous antibiotics to help clear it.

At the desk I could see one of the doctors and next to him was a lady wearing light coloured scrubs. I wasn't sure of her occupation, but she was a medic of some sort and it looked like they were discussing Bob's case. They both came over to speak to me and started to explain their concerns were increasing because Bob had still not responded within the expected timeframe. The doctor said it was possible that, given a little more time, along with visits from familiar people, the interaction would hopefully spark something in Bob's brain to help him wake up. His colleague/medic said she would observe Bob while family and friends visited him, and they would reduce sedation at the same time. She also said that if there were a lack of response it might indicate the brain stem had been affected. I began to feel anxious about what she had just implied, but I did feel that the doctor seemed more optimistic.

I knew the maximum visitors per patient was two to a bed, however I asked the doctor if it was possible for my three children and I to go in to see Bob together and he agreed. As I touched Bob's hand, I told him I was going to bring Jim, Mike, and Emma in next to see him. I knew it was going to be difficult to deliver the news to them and naturally as their mum, I wanted to be there to support them.

When I went back to the waiting room to see my children, Cheryl and Rab had arrived as well as Bob's mum and dad, sister, brother-in-law, and some of our closest friends. I briefly explained to everyone that Bob was still not responding, but we were hoping visits from everyone would help. I turned to my children and said "Ok, the doctor and his colleague have just spoken to me. They said that your dad is still not showing the response they would expect, so they want to observe Bob closely as we interact with him..." I couldn't help but notice how worried my children looked.

I continued, "They have agreed I can take you three in with me at the same time to see your dad. Afterwards, we will have to revert back to the two-visitor rule, so you will be able to go back in with your partners or on your own or both, whatever you feel is best for you. If anyone doesn't feel comfortable going in or you feel it's too much to handle, then that's ok. I'll understand."

My children hugged each other and then their partners and then I hugged them.

"Right, who wants to come in with me?" I asked.

"All three of us," they replied, and we were ready to go. I reminded them we were always told there were risks to the operation and that we also knew Bob would have certainly died without it. He had defied the odds on so many levels and we were not giving up without a fight. We had to give Bob a chance to respond.

I watched as the children stood by Bob's bedside. Emma was chatting away about the wedding plans, Mike was telling his dad about the new flat and Jim was giving updates on the football scores. They were all brilliant as they interacted with their dad but sometimes stayed silent as the monitors bleeped, watching for signs that their dad was responding in some way. I was so proud of them; it was humbling to see. I tried hard to hold back my tears as I saw each of them so desperately hoping for a response.

Mike was so excited when he held his dad's hand and asked him to squeeze it; he was convinced he felt a slight movement. Emma and Jim also did the same and said they noticed different things change on the monitors as they spoke to their dad. Charlie, Will and Lauren all agreed. Cheryl and Rab also felt that Bob was sensing their presence. Daphne, John, Julie, and Mitch were also trying to get a response from Bob and I was certain his heart rate increased as I and my children spoke to him.

Over the course of the next few days during these critical times, many of our close friends visited Bob and were convinced Bob could hear them. I was aware how hard it was for them to see him lying there motionless, all wired up to so many machines and monitors. Everyone was so supportive, not just to Bob but to me and the whole family. The love they had for Bob was so evident. I was extremely grateful they were visiting him, as I knew this could all help. We all wanted Bob to wake up! I was very moved by the way they all rallied round in this time of need.

Pete and Lisa were fantastic as they chatted to him. Pete was devastated when he first saw his best friend lying there in such critical condition. Nevertheless, he found the strength to overcome the initial shock. He told me they reminisced about the Norfolk holidays we had often shared. Our lovely friend Gwen also visited Bob and felt he could hear her. Gwen lived in the same village when our children were young, and our friendship had continued to grow over the years. Our families often shared many a Chinese takeaway and New Year's Eves.

Totty, my childhood best friend from school also came to see him. She was sure he knew she was there; I remember how upset she was. Tot was partly responsible for the reason Bob and I first met, but that's another story, and she was also one of my bridesmaids. Yet another much appreciated visitor was Kim. We first met each other at work many years ago and became friends. The nature of our job provided us with many skills to manage stressful situations and, as a duo, whether it be at work or in our personal lives, we had always seen each other through.

Another of Bob's dear friends who visited him was Pete, but nicknamed Smithy. He had known Bob since their early twenties when they both played for the same mixed hockey team. I would often watch Bob play his hockey matches and that's where I met Smithy and his lovely partner Felicity (Flis). We just hit it off straight away and have been good friends ever since.

There were even moments we found ways of laughing to help us all through it. Bob's friend and former work associate, Clive, had known him for years and they would often go on golfing holidays each year. Clive was devastated to hear about Bob. At the time, he was in Thailand but – the sign of a true friend - made urgent plans to fly back to the UK, heading directly from the airport to the hospital only to be told it was out of visiting hours and that only family could see Bob at this point. Clive being Clive proceeded to tell the staff he was Bob's older brother and was let in. When Daphne and John arrived at the hospital later that day, Clive could be heard saying, "Aww, there's Mum and Dad" before giving them a hug. They all laughed when Clive explained what he'd done! It was quite comical really, as there was a 12-year age gap between Bob and Clive and Clive was closer in years to Bob's parents than to Bob. Unlike Bob, Clive was a deeply religious man and prayed for him every day; although they were like chalk and cheese, they had a great friendship.

While family and friends continued to see Bob, I took the opportunity to visit St Luke's Chapel. It was the one I had noticed on the way in when Bob was first brought into Queen's. As I entered, I gazed at its beautiful décor. I saw a lovely picture of Jesus adorning the main wall and artificial candles glowing as their flames gently flickered. The chairs were set out in rows within the chapel and their upholstery was made of a soft velvet, which a deep burgundy colour. I noticed a prayer book and a pen that was placed on a table at the side of the room. As I opened it, I saw the many prayers people had written in it. I picked up the pen and then added my own prayer for Bob. I felt so peaceful as I sat down in the stillness. I could feel a profound sense of calm and renewed strength. It was the first of many times I would come to visit this chapel.

Returning to the Neuro unit, I went in to see Bob one last time before the visiting hours finished. I held Bob's hand and said, "Come on Bob, please open your eyes, you need to wake up. Emma is getting married in May and she needs her dad to walk her down the aisle." I was hoping this would resonate somewhere in his brain and spark a response. I kissed him on the cheek and said we would all be back to see him the next day. By this time, the medic who was observing had gone. I went back to the waiting room and managed to catch up with almost everyone who had seen Bob that afternoon. As we left the unit, we were discussing our experiences, and everyone was so sure that Bob could hear them. We were all on a high as we left the hospital that evening!

On our way home, I suggested to the kids that we order a takeaway for our evening meal and in the end we decided on a Chinese. It was all done with military precision: before you knew it, the brightly coloured flowers had been moved from the dining table to the unit in the corner of the open plan room, the cutlery and plates were placed on the dining table and the food warmers were ready with the candles already lit, just in time as the takeaway arrived. Once we had finished our meal, we gave the leftovers to Archie and Honey who were pleased with the egg fried rice and chicken chow mein. We cleared up the dishes and, with the dishwasher on, we sat down in the lounge. We were all feeling more optimistic about Bob as things looked like they were moving in the right direction.

We were all chatting about the past few days, out of the blue the greetings card on the rainbow flowers suddenly sprang from the bouquet and landed about two feet on the wooden floor in the lounge area. We all just looked at each other.

"That's a sign from my mum and dad," I said. They had passed away a few years earlier and they really loved Bob. I began to tell everyone about other spiritual signs including rainbows and even music and songs which Cheryl and I had both experienced while together at prominent times in our lives. Even a visit from a little red robin and a white feather that suddenly appeared and which I had always thought of as signs of hope. Whatever the outcome, they seemed to appear just at the right time to let us know that there is more to life and we are not alone.

We then went on to discuss the plans for the next day and how the children would juggle their work commitments.

As the hair salon wasn't open until Tuesdays, Emma had had time to arrange for colleagues to cover her appointments for the week ahead. She had only just recently switched from being an employee there to being newly self-employed. On the one hand, it meant she earned a higher wage, but on the other hand, if absent for any reason, she didn't receive an income. She was told that she still had to pay the weekly chair rent to the salon, which I thought was a bit harsh under the circumstances. We didn't even know if her dad would ever wake up and I didn't want her to have to worry about anything else, so I told her I would pay for it if needed, which I did. As her mum, I just wanted to protect her. Her partner, Will, worked for the local Council as a Community Caretaker at the time. When he had got the call from Emma on that Friday about her dad being critically ill, his boss had told him to go straight away. Will had phoned his boss to update on things and was told to take all the time he needed to support Emma and our family.

The headmistress at the school was very understanding and had already told Jim to take all the time he needed, especially given the seriousness of what had happened to his dad. His then future wife, Lauren, was also self-employed like Emma, running her own childminding business. I would have totally understood her need to go in to work, however, she was adamant that she wanted to stay and support Jim and the family. She had already contacted the parents of the children she looked after to let them know the nursery would be closed for the week ahead.

Mike worked for himself anyway and had set up a temporary office so he could work from mine. Mike's partner Charlie also wanted to stay to support us all; he managed the family-run tearoom and was able to organise cover.

There was no doubt that all of us wanted to see Bob again the following day without question but for now it was time for bed. Although Bob hadn't yet opened his eyes or woken up from the coma, the fact that we all felt Bob could hear us certainly eased our minds and we were all hopeful of sleeping better that night.

The following morning, on Monday 18th November, as we all sat around the table eating our breakfast, I called the Critical Care Unit to enquire about Bob. We were all hoping that Bob had woken up from the coma, although if he had, I would have thought the hospital would have called me by now.

As the call was answered a lady began to speak. "Hello" she said.

"Oh yes, good morning, it's Mrs Bloomfield, I'm calling to see how Bob is today please, is he showing any signs of response yet?" I asked.

She replied, "I'm really sorry, but Bob is still not responding despite everyone's best efforts. Are you and the family coming up to the hospital later?"

"Yes, we are" I replied.

"Ok, it might be better if we wait and have a chat once you arrive at the hospital and we can discuss my observations and options then." There was a pause as I hesitated.

"What do you mean by 'options'?" I asked.

"As Bob is not responding, we need to think about where we go from here," she said, her voice sounded quite dismal and sombre.

I couldn't be sure, and I really hoped I was wrong, but I got the feeling she was hinting there was no more that they could do for Bob. The 'options' or 'where we go from here,' may have meant addressing the issue of turning off his life support. I did think that wasn't something she would want to directly discuss over the phone.

I knew Bob's mum and dad would be up to visit Bob again that day with Julie and Mitch. However, I wanted to make them aware of the telephone conversation I'd just had with the medic. They confirmed they were coming up to the hospital straightaway and would see us there. I also left a message on Cheryl's answerphone. I knew she was at work, but if it were possible, I was sure Cheryl would come up to support me.

As I hung up, I could feel the energy in the room sink. I couldn't help but think about how this was affecting my children; the highs and lows of the past few days and the trauma of the whole ordeal was just so overwhelming. We had all felt so hopeful the day before and now all sorts of questions and scenarios and 'what ifs' began to race through our minds. What options did she mean? Maybe there was something else they could do? What if there was nothing more they can do? Was she suggesting turning off life support? What if Bob didn't wake up?

I suggested to the children and partners that we got to the hospital as soon as possible. I said, "We need to make extra time to give your dad a chance to respond. We need to see if there are still signs from him and we need to do that before we see the medic who has been observing him."

Chapter Five:

A Heartfelt Wish and Time to Let Go

Arriving at Critical Care, I buzzed the intercom. Although it wasn't within the official visiting hours, I asked if it would be possible for my children and I to see my husband. I was told that it would be. We decided I would go in first and the children would go in after.

On entering the unit, I glanced over towards Bob's cubicle. I could see a nurse standing at the foot of Bob's bed. I recognised him, he was the lovely kind young man called Rechel, who had asked me to bring in Bob's shaver and toiletries the day before.

"Good morning" I said.

"Oh, hi, Sue, I've just finished washing and shaving Bob and was just going over to the nurse's station to write up his notes, that's good timing. I'll give you some privacy, but I'll be about if you need anything."

"Thank you" I replied. I continued towards Bob's cubical. As I stood at his bedside, I could smell the Hugo Boss aftershave. I reached for Bob's hand and said hello to him and then leant over to give him a kiss. I have to say, Bob smelt absolutely gorgeous, and in that moment, I felt overwhelmed with emotion as teardrops began to cascade down my face.

You see, on previous visits it had always seemed so depersonalised, especially with Bob being attached to so many machines and monitors and everything always smelling so clinical, but that day it was different. Although Bob still remained unconscious and on the life support machine, the personal touch of applying Bob's aftershave made all the difference for me; in my eyes, that lovely young man had actually brought Bob back to life for a moment and I thank him so much for that! This is a memory I will never forget!

After chatting a while, I told Bob I loved him and then left the unit so my children and partners could go in next. As I came out of the double doors of Critical Care, my sister was waiting for me. She gave me a big hug and said she had told her boss she was leaving work to support me. I don't think she gave him a chance to say no! I told her to go in and see if she still thought Bob was responding in some way.

I asked Cheryl if she could stay with us when we discuss the next steps with the medic who had been observing Bob. It wasn't long before the lady arrived, and we were all seated in a little room, which was situated near Bob's cubicle. I was grateful that Cheryl was there with me. All of us were chatting and of the opinion that Bob could hear us and convinced he was still responding in some way. The medic disagreed and began to explain her thoughts on Bob's condition. She implied that the brain stem had been affected and was sure Bob was not showing any signs of response.

She continued, "Tests have been done to see if Bob can feel any pain. The results indicate that he has no response to pain. It appears his brainstem has been compromised and he is not showing any reactions or signs."

Mike began to challenge her opinion and said, "So, how do you explain the heart rate changes and the movement from him that I can feel when I ask him to squeeze his hand?"

"I'm sorry," she said, "his heart rate will fluctuate anyway and what you experienced was an involuntary movement from your dad. Bob had no control over that." Her tone seemed quite matter of fact.

She continued, "There is nothing else we can do for Bob. The tubes and machines seem to be the only things that are keeping him alive now." I remember Mike asked her again to clarify, she seemed quite adamant as she shook her head, "It was just an involuntary movement," she said.

I also wanted clarity and asked, "So, are you telling us Bob is brainstem dead and the machine is all that's keeping him alive?"

"Yes, I'm sorry," she replied.

We were given some time to digest the sad news and were told no decisions had to be made that day to turn off life support. Bob would remain in Critical Care where his family and friends were still able to see him. Naturally, we were all devastated and none of us wanted to believe it.

It was heart-breaking seeing my children and their partners so upset and we were all trying to console each other. We had just been told they believed Bob's brainstem was compromised, meaning damaged or dead, and there was nothing I could do to change the outcome for their dad. I had already tried so hard and, as their mother, I felt so helpless. I hugged each one of my children, their partners, and my sister, and prayed for the strength to help me and my children get through this.

Over the next few minutes, the family went back in to see Bob. The two-person rule went out the window and everyone was still trying to get him to respond: Cheryl was telling him to wake up; Emma refused to believe her dad would die so she and Will kept talking to him about their wedding, telling him she needed her dad to walk her down the aisle; Mike and Charlie were telling him to wake up and still asking him to squeeze their hands; Jim and Lauren told him that they wanted to start a family and their child would need a grandad.

We were aware that Daphne, John, Julie, Mitch, and Rab would be at the hospital by then, so we all walked into the waiting room where they were seated. As they looked at us, they could see we were all upset, and it became obvious it was sad news as we sat down and began to tell them what the medic had said. I explained that although no decision on timings had to be made today, they would need to discuss with us the process of turning off life support, but they would need me to consent first. For now, Bob would remain in Critical Care where anyone could still go in to see him if they wished.

My sister was a rock and so supportive. I didn't know it at the time, but Emma had told Cheryl she was going to cancel the wedding as she didn't want me to have the financial worry of paying for it. Cheryl told Emma not to cancel, saying her dad would want the wedding to go ahead and so would your mum. She recommended Emma waited and didn't do anything hasty. Cheryl didn't want to let me know what Emma had told her as she thought I was already dealing with so much. Unbeknown to me, Cheryl decided to approach John and informed him what Emma had said. He thanked Cheryl for letting him know and said he would sort it. He told Cheryl I was considered a big part of their family, and assured her the wedding would go ahead and the children and I wouldn't have to worry, as he and Daphne would make sure their daughter-in-law and their grandchildren were ok.

All of us continued to stay for a while, each of us taking turns to go back in and see Bob. As we walked through the corridor back to the unit, we saw another Doctor who was involved in Bob's care, I think he was more senior, and he stopped to talk to us. I asked him what would happen next in regard to discussing the process of turning off life support. I said Bob was already signed up to the organ donation register and, if it were possible, he would want to help others after his death.

His response was very unexpected. To my surprise, he said, "I wonder whether we should give Bob a little more time."

I looked at him totally puzzled; I wasn't sure if his colleague had updated him yet! "But your colleague has just told us there is nothing more that can be done!" I replied. I just couldn't take any more. I can recall every detail of that moment with perfect clarity as I stood in the corridor and raised my voice. "Right, I can't do this anymore, your colleague has just told us Bob's brainstem is compromised and the machine is the only thing keeping him alive. I even asked her to clarify it a second time. We all heard her say it, and we are trying to come to terms with it, and now you're telling us Bob may need more time!"

I could see the look on his face, he seemed quite taken aback. I continued "So, I suggest you have a chat with her and when you have made up your minds whether Bob's brainstem is compromised or not, then let me know, because I'm not coming up here anymore until you decide!"

I have to say, I'm normally more reserved than that, but with the emotions and intensity of the past few days running so high, I just flipped. It was extremely overwhelming for everyone. It had felt like we had all been stuck on a never-ending rollercoaster. One minute things looked promising, then the next our hopes were dashed. Then everything would just keep repeating back and forth with no end to it. I needed some space; it was time to go home.

Daphne and John were going to stay a bit longer to be with their son, so we said goodbye and that we would catch up later. It was late in the afternoon when we arrived home. We all felt so disheartened as we entered the bungalow, but the dogs were pleased to see us and it was lovely to be greeted with such unconditional love. After greeting the dogs, the kids made some drinks and I went into my bedroom to get my slippers and to take some time to reflect. As I sat down on the bed, I looked out of the window and I couldn't believe my eyes: in the sky was a double rainbow. I quickly called Jim and asked him to come outside. We went out the front door and I took a video to document it. I spoke, explaining things weren't looking good for Bob, but there was a beautiful rainbow, which was a great sign of hope and I asked Jim to speak and clarify the date 'Monday 18th November 2019.' This video is still on my phone to this day.

Even though I'd seen the rainbow, it did not necessarily mean that Bob would respond, it simply meant that whatever the outcome, things would be as intended. It was a sign I was not alone.

Later that afternoon, Will's mum came over to drop off some things for Will and Emma. Bob and I had met up often with Will's parents. In fact, the day before Bob collapsed, we had met Claire and Andy at a pub and had been discussing wedding plans. However, it seemed that day would now be very different. As Claire came into the kitchen area, I could see the tears in her eyes. She came straight over and gave me a big hug.

"I just can't imagine what you're going through, Sue, I'm so sorry." Both of us just hugged and no more words were needed. As she left, she gave us all another hug and said, "Please let me know if there is anything we can do to help."

That same evening, on the way back from the hospital, John and Daphne popped in to see us all. John told us they had spent some time with Bob and also spoke to one of the doctors in Critical Care, who had also told them unfortunately there was nothing more that could be done for their son as his brain stem was damaged. Obviously, we were all sad, but as a family we all stuck together and were discussing where we would go from there.

Later that night, I received a call from Critical Care. The children and their partners all stopped in their tracks. You could have heard a pin drop as I answered the call. It was one of the doctors calling to arrange a meeting with the family to discuss Bob. I was very blunt and told him it was not healthy for me or my family to keep going through so much uncertainty and I refused to come up to the hospital anymore until they had reached a decision about whether Bob was brain dead or not! Like I said, I was very blunt!

The doctor said he was aware of the discussion the family had with his colleague that day, but Bob had not shown any sign of response within the expected timeframe after a craniectomy procedure. He told us he would like to meet with the family to discuss this further and felt it would be better to do so in person, rather than over the phone. He said if we were coming up to see Bob tomorrow, he would be more than happy to meet with us on the ward to coincide with visiting hours if that helped, or we could arrange a specific time, whichever was easiest for us. So, I agreed we would meet with him on the following day to coincide with visiting Bob. I contacted Daphne and John to ask them if they wanted to be involved, which they did.

I mentioned to the children and to Bob's parents that, as I had power of attorney, the hospital would need me to consent to turning off Bob's life support. Obviously, we needed to discuss options at the meeting, but it would me who made the final decision about the next step and I would appreciate any opinions they felt they wanted to share with me. We would also see what the doctor had to say.

Speaking to my children, I said, "I know your dad's wishes and I know if there's a chance of a reasonable quality of life, we will all support him. However, if his brain and quality of life were severely impaired, he wouldn't want to live like that, so we have to do what is best for your dad, irrespective of how hard it could be for us."

The following day, Tuesday 19th November, the family met with the doctor on the Critical Care Unit. We were told the medic may have been a bit premature in suggesting it may be time to turn off Bob's life support. However, it had been another twenty-four hours and Bob was still not showing any signs of response, which suggested that his brainstem had indeed been compromised.

The doctor explained that normally they would expect a person who had undergone this type of brain surgery to have shown signs of response and be coming out of the coma by then, but unfortunately Bob was not. We were told that when the brainstem has been compromised and stops working, there is no chance of recovery and a person has effectively died, even though machines were keeping the body alive. The chances of Bob waking up were extremely unlikely.

Already knowing Bob's heartfelt wishes, I informed the doctor Bob was on the organ donation register and he would want to help others after his death, if it was possible. He said he would arrange for the organ donation team to contact me to discuss the process. Various meetings with the donor team were arranged to take place at Critical Care, and they were very considerate, combining those meetings to fit in with visiting times. This made it an easier process for the family, and everyone still had the opportunity to see Bob. So, while Emma and the rest of the family were visiting Bob, Jim, Mike, and I met with representatives from the organ donation team who were very respectful and explained the entire process. Emma didn't feel able to attend the meetings which I understood and respected. Emma was adamant and kept saying her dad was not going to die.

I asked what would actually happen when the time came to switch off life support. The lady explained we could play music and be with Bob to the end. Once Bob had passed away, we understood we would have to leave promptly, as they would need to prepare Bob's body for the organ donation recipients.

Even in this time of darkness, there were also comical moments. In particular, we were asked if Bob wanted to donate his corneas. Jim and Mike looked at me and the three of us just started laughing. The lady looked somewhat surprised, until I began to explain. Bob's eyesight was not good, and he wore contact lenses as he had actually previously received a corneal graft quite a few years ago. I joked it would be unlikely that they would pass quality control. However, it was lovely to think that in the same way that Bob had once been the recipient of someone's kind gift of sight, he would now be passing on special gifts to other people. Equally, his test results showed his kidneys and liver could be used to support another person's life. The valves in his heart looked ok and the results showed his heart was so good it might be possible to use for a whole heart transplant. However, to know for sure, more in-depth extensive tests would need to be done which would delay turning off life support for another day. Although this would be hard for us, we agreed for further tests to be done and a final meeting with the donation team was arranged to discuss results.

I remember the lady asked us if we wanted to remain anonymous or if the recipients wanted to get in touch would we be happy for them to contact us. It would be via her team anyway and I was happy to agree to this. I thought how lovely it would be if the person who received Bob's heart could come to the wedding, if it was possible. I would arrange for a stethoscope, so that Emma could hear her dad's heart beating on her wedding day, but then I had to stop thinking about it as teardrops began to form and roll down my cheeks.

On the day of the final meeting, as usual our family and close friends were also in the unit visiting Bob. With the paperwork signed, a date set, and everything explained, Mike, Jim and I thanked the lady and then made our way back to the waiting room. As we walked in, the room fell silent. I could see Will and Emma standing on the left-hand side against the wall, Lauren, Charlie, and Jim's best mate, Powelly, were gathered next to them. There was a row of seats to the right of the room where Bob's parents, Kim, Julie, and Mitch were seated. Cheryl and Rab were sitting at the back of the room next to the water dispenser. On entering the room, I took a deep breath. I have no idea how I managed it, but I began to explain.

I told everyone that there was nothing else we could do for Bob except follow his known wishes. Friday 22nd November 2019 was the day we would have the opportunity to say our final goodbye to Bob. Everyone was welcome to do that, but I would understand if it was too much for some people. The team had said we were all able to be together at Bob's bedside, where we could talk to him, hold his hand, even play music if we wanted and stay with him until the end. Once Bob had passed away, we would have to leave promptly as they would need to prepare his body for the organ donation recipients.

It was a very upsetting time for us all with so many mixed emotions. There had always been two possible outcomes: Bob could have survived or not and, although it wasn't the outcome we wanted, it gave us some sense of relief. The last few days had been so mentally and emotionally challenging for us all and we were no longer stuck in limbo, but it also came with such deep sadness as it meant we would soon have to say goodbye to Bob.

Emma, Will, Jim, Lauren, Mike, and Charlie were so upset; even through our own sadness, Cheryl, Kim, and I were trying so hard to console them all. I will never forget how Will and Powelly sobbed, both telling me Bob was like a dad to them. Bob's official name was Robert. Lauren and Jim told me about wanting to start a family and, as a tribute and in memory of Bob, if they had a boy, they would give him Robert as a middle name. I was so touched by this.

Daphne looked so sad as she sat there cradling her arm and wiping away the tears with her hankie. I remember John told me he felt like kicking the wall, saying it should be him, not his son. I could see he was trying to remain strong for everyone. Mitch looked upset and was trying to hold his tears back while Julie just appeared blank, staring at the floor in disbelief. None of us could really believe this was happening. I think some people went back in to see Bob again, still trying so desperately to get him to respond before leaving the hospital to go home.

At the time, my other sister, Allie, was away in America with her family on a holiday of a lifetime and we hadn't said anything to them up to this point as we didn't want to spoil their holiday, given that there wasn't much they could do anyway. However, now things had changed, and it was the day before they were due to travel home, the decision was made to inform them. This gave them an opportunity to see Bob to say goodbye if they wanted to.

I knew I would need to let other members of my family and friends know to give them the opportunity to visit Bob one last time, but I was so upset, I just couldn't bring myself to make the calls, so Rab took my phone and kindly made those calls for me. I knew it was difficult for him, because as he returned, I could see he had been crying too.

I went back in to see Bob again before I left to go home. As I looked at him, with so many tears streaming down my face, I felt so distraught at the thought of life without him. To see my children and everyone else go through so much was heart-breaking. It seemed there was nothing else I could do for Bob; I knew his heartfelt wish and it was time to let go. I had to accept Bob would not survive and to follow his known wishes. I would now need to focus on my children and support them through one of the toughest times in our lives.

Later that evening, Daphne and John popped in to see us. Obviously, we were all distraught, but as a family we all stuck together. It was then I learnt of Emma's plans to cancel the wedding as John had spoken with her about this. He had told her that in no way was she to cancel it, as he would take care of things. The planning of the wedding had all been organised but obviously Emma was still thinking she would be facing the day without her dad. It was quite emotional as she asked her grandad if he would give her away and walk her down the aisle. We knew Bob had already written his speech and Mike had searched the files on Bob's computer and found it, but it was password protected. However, Mike soon figured out the code. We all read the speech apart from Emma. It was so lovely and we all agreed it would be a fitting tribute for John to read Bob's speech on Emma and Will's wedding day.

John also said he would speak to Bob's colleagues about his work, as they would need to discuss Bob's role and agree on various matters since Bob owned joint shares in the building company. Plans were made for John, Mike, and Jim to attend a meeting with Bob's fellow directors on my behalf. John was also helpful in giving me some financial advice, but I wasn't sure if I could afford to stay in the bungalow on my own. When someone dies it changes your whole situation: you still have the outgoings of bills etc. but now only one income. At the time, I did not want to think about that, but once losing Bob was imminent, I reluctantly had to.

I wondered if I would need to sell the bungalow and how I would manage with the household jobs and maintenance Bob would normally do. Jim wanted to help and reassure me, so he did a spreadsheet on financial incomings and outgoings. I would now need to organise the admin side of things, the bills, utilities, and insurance, as this was something Bob had always done, and I would need to learn to do this myself now, as well as dealing with the grief of losing Bob.

We would also have to think about the funeral. John said he would speak to his friend Ernie, who was a recently retired funeral director. John offered to liaise and help with the funeral arrangements. It might seem in retrospect that it was a bit early to think of such things, but everyone deals with grief differently and I think John needed a focus; he is a very practical man and wanted to support his son's family by making himself useful.

That evening, I sent Daphne and John an email, saying how lovely their son was and what a great dad and husband he had been. I also thanked them for all the support they had shown to me and my family throughout the years. I was very touched when I received a lovely and very moving reply, which meant a lot to me. Daphne and John are quite reserved in some ways and, although I knew I was always well respected by them, it was lovely to learn just how much I meant to them.

On Thursday 21st November, the day before the children and I would have to turn off Bob's life support, everyone had the opportunity to visit Bob one last time and many of our family and friends went to say their final farewells. Cheryl and Rab popped in to see me on their way home and we discussed the plans for the following day. They said that they would drive us to the hospital as they understood it would be a difficult thing we would be doing. They felt we didn't need the pressure of driving back after such an ordeal, so I agreed to call them in the morning with a time to collect us.

That evening, I double checked with Daphne and John to see if they wanted to be there with us tomorrow when we said our final goodbye to Bob. John said it would be too much for Daphne to cope with and they, along with Julie and Mitch, had already said their goodbyes. I then checked with my children and partners whether they were ok to go, I would understand if they felt it would be too hard for them. However, they all said they wanted to be there. I was so relieved, as I did not want to do this alone. We would wait for the phone call in the morning confirming that everything was in place, that the organ donation team was on site and ready, as well as the organ donor recipients. Once everything had been coordinated, we would receive a call to come into the hospital to be with Bob at the end of his life, before he gave the gift of a new life to others. It was Bob's heartfelt wish and time to let go.

At the thought of what lay ahead the following day, I started to feel very anxious and decided to take some Calms to help me relax a bit. I knew that night would be a difficult one and that my children were trying not to show how upset they were. They were trying to protect me and be strong for me and I was trying to do the same for them. I was totally exhausted, the emotions that came with knowing we would be saying goodbye to Bob soon and the strength it took to stay strong for my children and Bob's parents was immense. I didn't think much about me; my children took priority and I ploughed all my energy into doing my best for them.

As we went to bed, I knew there would be tears behind closed doors. Lauren told me a few days later that Jim cried himself to sleep and I'm sure he wasn't alone in doing so. When I closed my bedroom door, I just fell to my knees, sobbing. Through the many tears, I prayed with all my heart and soul, "Please God, please help us, I don't want to be a widow and my children don't want to lose their dad, please help us."

PART II
Praying for a Miracle

Chapter Six:

In the Blink of an Eye

Friday 22nd November 2019 would be the toughest day of my life and one nothing could have ever prepared me for. I would be saying goodbye to my husband and supporting my children to say goodbye to their dad. I knew that in my own grief I would still need to remain strong to support my children in theirs.

As I waited for the telephone call from Queen's to confirm the time we would need to arrive, I began to think about how my life would be without Bob. There were a lot of thoughts running through my head that morning. I began to wonder how my children and I would cope with the loss of their dad. We have always been such a close family and losing Bob would be like losing the engine of a car; he was the heart of our family. But I knew without a doubt I had done absolutely everything I possibly could have done for him and I also knew Bob couldn't remain in a coma, being kept alive by the life support system. We couldn't just stay as we were in this black void forever.

The past couple of weeks had been mixed with all sorts of emotions and immense stress for everyone. Although this day would be tinged with great sadness, we needed closure and I had come to terms with having to let Bob go and had accepted this.

We received the telephone call to say everything was coordinated, the recipients of the organs and the organ donation team were ready. A time had been scheduled for my family and I to be with Bob in his last moments. I telephoned Cheryl to let her know and arranged for her and Rab to pick us up and take us to the hospital. There are some things I remember so clearly from this day and some things that I don't. I remember Cheryl and Rab arriving at the bungalow, each had driven their own cars to accommodate us all. I remember Cheryl and Rab hugging us all as they came in. I also remember telling my children that if they felt unable to come, they didn't have to, or if when we got to the hospital they felt they could not go in to see their dad, I would understand. Jim, Mike, Emma, Lauren, Charlie, and Will were all adamant they would be by my side throughout the whole process.

As we all got ready to leave, I gave Archie and Honey a big hug and a treat, and I think we took a few bottles of water from the fridge for the journey. I was feeling very apprehensive, fearful, and anxious at what was to come. As we left the house, I grabbed the keys, closed the door and locked up, then began walking towards the cars.

As unbelievable as it sounds, as we left the house that day to start the final journey, another beautiful vibrant and colourful rainbow appeared in the sky above my home. Everyone saw it and, although I had already noticed it, my children made sure I knew as they all pointed it out to me. Cheryl and Rab were amazed, in fact we all were. I knew that God was with me and it gave me great comfort and hope.

I sat in the front passenger seat of Cheryl's car, as Will and Emma had already taken the back seats. Charlie said he would drive Mike in their car and Lauren and Jim joined Rab in his. As we all got settled into the vehicles ready to travel in convoy once more, we fastened our seatbelts and prepared to leave. Cheryl turned on the ignition, and the car radio started playing Angels by Robbie Williams. Cheryl and I both looked at each other, we knew this was another spiritual sign, as we had both experienced something similar when our mum and dad passed away and indeed many more signs besides.

Having already shared some of my experiences of spiritual signs with my children and their partners a few days earlier, coupled with the rainbows we had all seen, I felt they were open to this, so I phoned Jim and then Mike, to tell them about the Angels song and asked them to put Magic Radio on and listen to the songs that play, some of which might be relevant to you and your dad. It did transpire later when we spoke about it that some of the songs were relevant, but more for me and Cheryl as there were so many connected to our mum and dad.

With all of us now on the road, Cheryl was leading the convoy as we drove through Colchester to join the A12 following the rainbow as we went. Cheryl glanced in her rear view mirror every now and again to check Rab and Charlie were still following behind us. In our car, everyone was quiet just listening to the music. The traffic was flowing at a steady pace and we had plenty of time to arrive at our destination.

I can remember looking up through the passenger side window at the light blue sky and could see a hint of the morning sun hiding behind a fluffy white cloud. I noticed a smoky trail from the engines, where airplanes had once flown, and I could see where their paths had crossed over. There were quite a few trails that formed many shapes of an X. It looked like a lot of kisses had been written in the sky, just like a picturesque postcard from heaven. 'How lovely!' I thought.

As we continued on our journey, I began to feel a renewed strength and real sense of calmness around me. All of my fear had left, I wasn't scared at the prospect of saying goodbye to Bob anymore, but I didn't know why. It felt like there were a thousand angels wrapping their wings around me and I felt guided in some way.

We had been traveling for quite a while and had a little way to go before we would reach Queen's. Suddenly, my phone started to ring. It was the hospital.

"Oh, no, it's the hospital" I said. I remember wondering if they were calling to say Bob had already passed away! Cheryl turned down the volume on the radio and I answered the call.

"Hello, Sue speaking."

"Oh hello, I'm the consultant from Critical Care, is that Mrs Bloomfield?"

"Yes, its Sue, Bob's wife, is everything ok?"

"Sue, I'm ringing to let you know we're not sure we are able to go ahead with the organ donation, have you left home yet?"

"Yes, we are about twenty minutes away from arriving at the hospital." I replied.

"Ok, it might be best to wait and talk to you once you arrive here," he said.

"Erm, no, I don't think so, you can't just leave me not knowing what this is about. Why can't we go ahead?" I asked.

The consultant continued, "We believe Bob is responding with his eyes."

"Are you sure?" I said.

He continued, "Yes, we believe he is trying to, so, when you arrive at the hospital come straight to Critical Care, Bob will still be there."

"Ok, thank you," I said.

I looked at Cheryl and then turned to Emma and Will. In a surprised and uncertain tone I said, "They think he's responding with his eyes." All of us were totally shocked, we couldn't believe it and then began to express our excitement and joy with a nervous but happy kind of laugh.

"I need to phone Jim and Mike to let them know," I said. I immediately phoned Jim, he answered cautiously. "Jim, you're not going to believe this, I've just received a call from the consultant, they think your dad is responding with his eyes." Jim was so excited and told Lauren and Rab and then I heard the cheers and joy in the background. Emma and Will looked out of the back window of the car and could see Rab, Jim and Lauren smiling, they all signalled a thumbs up to each other. I then phoned Mike and again there was a sense of disbelief, but so much joy. Everyone was so happy.

As we continued the journey, there were a lot of questions running through my head and this naturally came with some uncertainty. I couldn't be sure or know what to expect, but it would be lovely for Bob to respond and open his eyes and to be able to understand and communicate. However, if it turned out he was severely impaired, mentally or physically, I knew he wouldn't want to live like that and if this were the case, I would feel like I had failed him in his wishes. The impact this would have on the entire family would be massive.

I wondered if they were right, was Bob really responding? But, then, it certainly was a big call to halt organ donation. Surely they had to truly feel Bob was trying to respond with his eyes in some way to call it all off? I also couldn't dismiss the many rainbows and signs I had seen so far, and I knew although my head had many questions, my heart would guide me.

My thoughts then moved to all the people that had been bleeped to go to the hospital, thinking they would be receiving a vital organ transplant and another chance of a better life, but now that had all been paused. It was a bittersweet moment and, even though I had no idea who these people were, I did feel for them and their families.

Before I knew it, we had arrived at Queen's. As we parked up and got out of our cars, we all gathered in a big circle, embracing each other. We were so happy and excited at the prospect of Bob responding. I was pleased to see my children so happy, but I also wanted to err on the side of caution, so before we went any further I spoke to everyone and said all we knew at this point was that they thought there was a response but that there had been doubts and conflicting information before. I was sure that when we saw him, we would know what to think. I needed to prepare everyone just in case.

The walk from the car park into the hospital was a bit of a blur, the adrenaline was running so high, but I do remember we all made a beeline for Critical Care, and nothing was going to stop us! After buzzing the intercom on the double doors, we were let in and all of us walked over to Bob's cubicle. The consultant joined us and stood on the far side of Bob's bed while Jim, Lauren, Mike, Charlie, Emma, Will, Cheryl, and Rab, were all standing with me on the other side. Nurses were also observing from the desk.

As expected, Bob still needed help from the life support machine and, just like before, the tubes remained in his mouth and airways to help him breathe. I remember how peaceful he seemed, as he lay there with his eyes closed. In that moment, I silently prayed for a miracle, hoping he would respond. I recall how everyone remained so quiet as I called his name…

"Bob!"

I only had to call him once. Straight away he opened those big blue eyes!

On that day, Friday 22nd November 2019 in the blink of an eye and rainbows high, from a stroke to critical, we all witnessed a miracle!

It was just so unbelievable; you could hear everyone in the room gasp. We were all so happy. Tears of joy could be seen flowing down everyone's faces. The relief that Bob had woken up from the coma was immense. Still, he remained attached to life support with various tubes in his airways and throat, and wouldn't be able to talk. I was also aware it was possible his speech could be affected by the stroke. It was certainly good he had opened his eyes on hearing his name, but I needed more! I had never experienced or seen anything quite like this before and I had no idea how I should speak to or communicate with someone responding from a coma. But I needed to know what capacity Bob had to understand things and the only way to do that was to test him.

"Bob, it's Sue, can you hear me?" I said. I was holding his hand and said, "Squeeze my hand if you can hear me." Bob did, he squeezed my hand, it was very subtle, but he did it. My heart was racing. I wanted to see if he could do something different, so then I asked him, "Bob, blink your eyes." Bob did, he blinked his eyes. This was absolutely incredible!

I desperately needed to see if we could communicate in some way, so I explained this to him and asked him, "Bob blink once for yes." Bob did, he blinked once for yes. Then I said, "Bob blink twice for no," but Bob only blinked once this time, and I wasn't sure if he could understand me, but after a moment, he blinked again. There had been a few seconds delay, but I knew he understood. Just to double check I asked him again to blink twice, but this time I knew to give him a few seconds extra to blink again and he did, he blinked twice. I told him that blinking twice meant no. I asked him if he understood, he blinked once, indicating 'Yes.' Finally, I asked him to clarify the sign for 'no,' and he blinked twice.

I was elated, we were able to communicate, I knew he could hear and understand. I could feel my heart expanding as Bob was able to respond. Then I asked the question I was dreading the most, "Are you in any pain, Bob?" he blinked twice indicating 'No.'

All of us were ecstatic, there were tears of absolute joy. Although at this point, Bob could not move the rest of his body, I knew that he could understand, and I knew that somehow everything would be ok. I had rainbows and I had hope! I had a fantastic family and brilliant friends and I had Bob............ Bob was back!

I knew everyone would be expecting a call to say Bob had passed away. I wanted his parents and everyone to know that Bob had woken up and was responding. I also wanted to stay with Bob and my family, so I gave my phone to Rab and asked him to make the calls for me. This time he had good news to share!

Once Rab had finished calling everyone, he came back into critical care to return my phone and joined the rest of us to be with Bob. It wasn't long before my phone started to ping with text message notifications from our close friends. Pete and Lisa were thrilled at the news along with Smithy, Flis, Gwen, Totty, Kim, and Clive. Obviously, I wanted to respond and keep everyone updated, but to do this individually would prove to be time consuming and I needed to focus my time on Bob.

Emma came up with a great idea and immediately set up a WhatsApp group chat. This meant we could add all our family and friends to it. Everyone could collectively receive updates and post their own messages within it. It bought us all together in one place. Emma aptly named it 'Team Bob.'

And so, the beginning of Team Bob was created…

Chapter Seven:

Team Bob

November 2019

As soon as family and friends received notification that they had been added to the 'Team Bob' WhatsApp group, it wasn't long before loads of messages came flooding in. Here is a copy of part of the transcript including times and date of some of the messages sent on the day that Bob responded.

*[22/11/2019, 13:56:44] **Emma:** created group "Team Bob"*

*[22/11/2019, 16:37:26] **Sue:** Team Bob Thank you everyone for all your support today. Day1communications through eyes by blinking. Bob is comfortable and now resting, so we are now leaving the hospital but will keep you all updated on here.*

*[22/11/2019, 16:59:46] **Flis & Smithy:** Thankyou Sue for updating us. It's hard for you to communicate with us all, this is a fabulous group to set up. Sending heartfelt positive thoughts to you all xxxxx*

[22/11/2019, 17:59:02] **Pete:** *It is a fabulous group chat and to be part of 'Team Bob' What has happened today is truly amazing 👍 xxxx 🌈*

[22/11/2019, 18:20:17] **Lisa:** 👍♥ 🌈

[22/11/2019, 18:41:17] **Clive:** *Hello Team Bob Thank you for including me I am very honoured It will be lovely to see Bob's blue eyes shining again Bringing us his love.*

[22/11/2019, 19:35:29] **Julie:** *It's very appropriate Lisa has put a rainbow 🌈 as this morning as I drove over the Strood, on the way to Mums to await the news that he has passed away, there was a very bright rainbow and I said to Mitch whenever I see a rainbow, I will think of Robert going to heaven. Now I think the rainbow wasn't complete and it was Robert getting halfway there and decided he didn't want to go. Can't believe how today has turned out.*

[22/11/2019, 21:17:17] **Jim:** *Just to update you all... I rang the hospital. He is still responding through eye movements. Also, his blood pressure has come down which is positive. He is not complaining of any pain. x.*

[22/11/2019, 21:29:59] **Sue:** *I plan to go tomorrow aim to get there about 3.00pm.*

[22/11/2019, 21:35:10] **Lisa:** *Pete and I will visit Bob Tuesday afternoon about 4.00pm.*

[22/11/2019, 21:55:03] **Jim:** *Lauren and I will go tomorrow morning about 8am x.*

[22/11/2019, 21:57:17] **Charlie:** *Me and Mike will go Sunday afternoon x.*

[22/11/2019, 22:02:28] **Cheryl:** *I can go Tuesday/Wednesday at 3.30pm.*

[22/11/2019, 22:53:16] **Powelly:** *Me & Jim are going next Saturday, just before my Wedding. See if Bob thinks I'm making the right decision* 😄*! x*

[22/11/2019, 23:39:56] **Sue:** *Remember one blink for YES, two blinks for NO*

The next day, Saturday 23rd November, I had an extraordinarily strong feeling Bob would be successful in this fight and that morning whilst I was on my laptop, a YouTube music video popped up and started playing this particular song 'It's Going to Be All Right' by Sara Groves. The song touched me deeply and the video had many inspiring pictures and life quotes, so I posted the link on 'Team Bob.'

Saturday [23/11/2019] **Sue:** *It's going to be alright! https://www.youtube.com/watch?v=vmzo3KxP5wo*

If you enter this into your web browser, hopefully it will still be there to view.

Over many weeks Bob received daily visits from family and friends and more and more people were added to 'Team Bob.' It enabled all members to feedback and liaise with medical teams on any updates or enquiries about Bob's care needs during their visits. This book holds just a snippet of the many messages, updates and dialogue that were posted by the group's members. They also help to tell Bob's story and give a clear record and timeframe of Bob's recovery from their perspectives.

It was an invaluable way of communicating with everyone, which played a vital part in keeping Bob moving forward. Without a doubt, I am sure this helped his progress and the speed at which things began to improve! It was key in keeping Bob healthy, overseeing his recovery, and keeping his brain active to help reconnect the parts of it affected by the stroke. It clearly shows the importance of working as a team.

Even now, as I look back on these, I am reminded of how amazing Bob's progress was and the importance of the constant love, support, care, and time given to Bob, which is reflected in so many other messages within the Team Bob WhatsApp group. Although I am unable to include every message within this book, I believe all of them deserve a place here!

Saturday [23/11/2019] Day after responding.

Jim: *Just seen Dad. He was very tired but still able to communicate through his eyes. Occasionally his bottom jaw moved but he was unable to do this on command. The doctor said it is probably a reflex action or that he is uncomfortable with the intubation tube in his mouth. Overnight he communicated that he was in a little pain, so was given pain relief and is now pain free. This is good as he can feel pain. He was trying very hard to keep his eyes open the whole time that we were there. As we left, I watched him, and he closed his eyes once we were out of his eyeline. We don't know if he can remember things, so I think it's important for visitors to explain where he is and what has happened. Also tell him the time and to sleep when you are leaving x.*

Kim: *It's a miracle Sue.*

Sunday [24/11/2019]

Julie: *Visited Robert with Mum and Dad. He kept his eyes open the whole time didn't get a smile but when the nurse asked him to wriggle his toes he did!! Thank you Flis and Smithy for getting up REALLY early to enable my Mum and Dad to have some alone time with him.*

Mike: *Dad did really well and was able to nod yes to me and Charlie on a couple of occasions. He is now going to have a CT scan and they asked if it was ok to sedate him and he said yes.*

Monday [25/11/2019]

Emma: *Dad is moving both feet and when we got there the nurse said he keeps trying to cross his legs and does do that on his own and can squeeze both hands very lightly. He had some head movements, and it looks like he is trying to laugh at things I say. Just to let you all know they are now doing one blink for yes and eyebrow raise for no. But you have to keep reminding him as I think he forgets. He said he had no pain and looks pretty good considering. I opened the card for him from Smithy and Flis and asked if it was them who got him the rubber duck and he blinked for yes! X*

Flis & Smithy: *He remembered!!! 🦆!!! He smiled when we gave it to him! We gave the calendar to him too which the nurse said they will turn daily for him!*

Will: *Bob now shakes his head for no, kept pointing at nurse when he wanted her. Emma asked about his breathing and every breath is his own – the tube only for support if needed. Doing really well and was pleased to see us! We stayed longer than we thought as he didn't want us to leave. He was also doing a thumbs up at the end too! x*

Things were going well with Bob and everyone was feeling more positive about the future. My children had been brilliant, it had been a great comfort having them stay with me, however, I was aware they would need to return to work at some point and back to their own homes, so over the next couple of days the kids moved out.

With everyone wanting to see Bob, it soon became necessary to stagger visits so as not to tire him out. I decided to ask Bob's sister if she would organise a visiting rota, where everyone could book allocated slots. Julie posted a visiting chart within Team Bob, which worked really well. This ensured Bob had at least one visitor every day. It also gave me a bit of a break as I hadn't realised until this point how exhausted I had become, especially with the constant visits to and from the hospital.

The lack of time for myself was starting to have an impact on my own mental health and wellbeing. It had been a hard few days and the adrenalin that had been constantly keeping me fighting had gradually left my body. Everything that had happened finally caught up with me and I was still finding it hard to sleep. As my mind became tired, I began to lose myself; having been constantly under so much stress, uncertainty and pressure, the serotonin levels in my brain began to plummet. Having worked in the mental health sector, I was aware of the need to see my GP and I knew I needed to remain well to continue to support Bob and my family. The following morning, I went to see my doctor who prescribed me some medication to help get my serotonin levels back to normal and to help me sleep. I also needed time to rest away from the hospital for a couple of days. I remember feeling so guilty that I wasn't well enough to see Bob, but I needed to take time to heal from the trauma and I knew family and friends were visiting Bob, which gave me great comfort. I also had the WhatsApp chat with all the updates and could see how well he was doing.

My closest friends were supporting me in different ways, checking in on me, talking things through and spending time with me. I remember this was the first time I felt able to release all the emotion that I had been holding inside, I hadn't allowed myself to really breakdown or cry until now. This was when good friends helped me to carry the load; I will be forever grateful to them. They were all very kind, making sure I was eating ok, some turning up with my favourite takeaway and lovely flowers to brighten my day.

It was lovely to have the time to get back to walking the dogs again and it felt good to be out in the cool fresh air. Honey and Archie were also a great comfort and their cuddles on the sofa were a regular tonic. After some much-needed rest and the medication quickly taking effect in my system, it wasn't long before I was back to my old self and able to visit Bob again. Family and friends also continued their visits and Bob's secretary, Pat, coordinated a rota - with help from Julie - for planned visits from Bob's work colleagues.

Tuesday [26/11/2019]

Pat: *Morning everyone. Wonderful to read all these positive messages. Colleagues from work would love to join me on a visit to see Bob one morning. Inundated with calls every day Sue. People so concerned about Bob. I miss him so much here. Keeps everyone calm!*

Rab: *Hi all I have been humbled by the love and support that you all have been giving, with all your hearts, giving positive love, thoughts, and prayers to Bob and the family. My honest opinion is that Bob felt the Love from all on here and from far and wide which resulted in him showing the positive response he did, all be it leaving it very late, but we all know he's full of surprises. The love, caring, and the positiveness was shining through from every one of us like a big rainbow and Bob caught the middle of it. He let us all know that he was back fighting, everybody who was on their way to the hospital on Friday morning witnessed that and when we got there, we all saw the fight in his eyes. I believe him seeing Sue, Jim, Michael, his lovely daughter Emma, Lauren, Charlie and Will all willing him on, opened the fire in his belly even more as he turned it into the fight back. We all know he has a long fight ahead and mustn't lose sight of that, but he knows that every one of us is standing by his side with all our support and affection and are all fighting with him. Keep the faith!*

Mike: *I've given Dad an iPad that's in his drawer now. I've connected it to premium Wi-Fi so instructions to connect are inside. If he's not too tired perhaps when people leave, they can play* *something for him.*

Emma: *Spoke to the doctor. Basically, they want to wait a few more days to see if his breathing improves, he can breathe on his own but it's not as strong as they need. They don't want to leave the tubes down his throat so will see if it improves in a few days, if not, they will do a tracheostomy. The doctor said since Dad had woken up, he has progressed quicker than people normally would. His glasses are there. So just ask him if he wants them on. It helps him to see his iPad screen and also in the distance if people come to see him. x*

Wednesday [27/11/2019]

Will: *Bob has had drain removed from his skull today as not much fluid was coming out. They think he has a chest infection and waiting on results back from the lab. Everything else is still the same and positive. Nurse is encouraging Bob to move his legs which he's doing when told but is very tired. He is stronger with his legs especially his right one.*

Cheryl: *He moved his left arm and is trying to sit up using his shoulders he can move his legs, looks like he can move right leg at the top. Left him comfortable he was tired. I gave him a kiss and said we all love him. He squeezed my hand. x*

Thursday [28/11/2019]

Pat: *So lovely to see our friend this morning. Communicating well with eyes and lots of thumbs up. He was trying to impress me with his feet movement - asked if he was doing an Irish jig, and I got another thumbs up. Nurse said he slept well through the night. Bob shook his head when asked if he was in any pain.*

Jim: *Dad has shown me all his tricks. The nurse said she doesn't think he has a chest infection, or he'd be on antibiotics by now. I put the iPad on for him and he moved his hand right to his face and pointed. I said do you want your glasses and he gave a thumbs up. Leaving now as they're going to remove the second half of the stitches in his head which have healed nicely. I asked if he remembered seeing me earlier in the week, he blinked yes. He also thinks his short and long-term memory is okay. I put my hand on his arms, shoulders, legs, and face and asked if he could feel me touching him and he blinked for yes x.*

Powelly: *Love this mate. What a legend!!!*

Julie: *I spoke to Wiggy who visited this afternoon, and he said the nurse told him that Bob's recovery has been phenomenal so far. Wiggy is an old friend and work colleague from the boat building company where they use to work together.*

Clive: *What an amazing team of people and the amazing link is Bob. A miracle! What a guy!!!*

Friday [29/11/2019] One week after responding.

Emma: *Dads blood pressure has come right down now. Speech and language therapist said he finds it hard to move his eyes side to side, if we show him anything we should do it so he only has to move his eyes up and down. He has double vision which is normal because he hasn't worn his contacts or glasses for so long! He told them he wanted his glasses and picked magic radio station on iPad. Dad's breathing is stronger than the machine pretty much all of the time, but he did have a blip the other night when it wasn't. But most of the time his breathing is stronger. The nurse said he's doing really well! I was talking about wedding plans and Dad walking me up the aisle, she said he's fighting because he wants to be there x.*

Saturday [30/11/2019]

Lauren: *Bob lifted his hand to wave as we came in. He blinked all the responses for his football league Super 6 scores. He did thumbs up when talking about Powelly's wedding (I'm going to film some to show him Monday) We put radio on for him and he was tapping his toes along to the music. When we left Bob squeezed our hand and gave us a thumbs up (right side), whoever visits this afternoon please bring Bob shower gel & shaving foam. Thanks. x.*

Clive: *Great to see Bob today, shower gel and shaving foam restocked. I miss him so much Can't wait to have a San Miguel together.*

December 2019

Sunday [01/12/2019]

Flis & Smithy: *Well Bob is looking and doing so well. It's incredible how much of an improvement he's making on a daily basis. Definitely responding to Smithy's humour!! Well done Team Bob. x*

Gwen: *It was so good to see Bob this afternoon. He was showing me his toe wiggling & gave me several thumbs up. I'm sure he'll go from strength to strength; his determination will see to that. Everyone's visits must, I'm sure, be helping too xx*

I was pleased that Flis and Gwen had scheduled a visit for Bob that day because Jim, Lauren, Emma, and I were attending Powelly's wedding, so we weren't able to see him. Jim was best man and Bob and I had previously been invited to attend. Even though Bob couldn't be there, I knew he wanted me to go and Powelly had arranged for Emma to attend with me on Bob's behalf.

The day was lovely, and I did enjoy it, although there were moments where I found myself getting a little tearful as the whole concept of the wedding reminded me of my own and subsequently thoughts of Bob. But it was great to see Powelly so happy on his big day, needless to say. Bob must have given him the thumbs up when Powelly visited and asked him if he was doing the right thing!

It was really nice to spend time with Lauren and Emma, especially away from the hospital environment, and we even managed a few steps on the dance floor. Jim did a fantastic job as best man and I was also touched by Powelly's speech as he wished Bob well when asking everyone to raise a glass for the toast. It was lovely to see how Jim's mates were all supporting him too. The following day was Jim's birthday. While at breakfast we all sang Happy Birthday to him. Once we had checked out of the hotel, we drove to the hospital to see Bob.

Monday [02/12/2019]

Jim: *Just seen Dad with Lauren and Mum. He is doing well. We showed him Powelly's wedding photos, and I got a thumbs up for my wedding speech. He did his football Super 6 predictions and squeezed everyone's hand and waved, he moved his hand up and called me over when he was uncomfortable, and we found it was because he was hot - which we soon fixed. Big news is that tomorrow the breathing tube is coming out. If he is able to swallow his saliva afterwards then that will be great. If not, they will fit a tracheostomy tube to help remove any build-up of saliva. Either way he will have the freedom of his mouth and be much more comfortable x*

Powelly: *Great birthday present for you Jim, to see your dad and have great news as well x.*

The following day I received a call to go up to the hospital as they needed me to sign a consent form for a tracheostomy. They explained that Bob's breathing tube had been removed, but he was having a few problems clearing his throat. On arrival, I greeted Bob and explained that he needed to have a tracheostomy and asked if he was ok with this, which he agreed to. So, I signed the consent form on his behalf. I was told the procedure would take about 30 minutes and was scheduled to be done for about 3.00pm, by which time I'd have to be making my way back home, so I decided I would call them later to see how it had gone, although I had every faith it would be ok.

It had taken about an hour to get back home as the traffic was heavy that day, so I decided to call the hospital to see if everything had gone to plan. The nurse looking after Bob said the tracheostomy was done at his bedside under sedation, all went well with no complications. He is comfortable and awake. She informed me Bob was now on the General Intensive Therapy Unit (ITU) which was located just past the Critical Unit.

As Bob clearly had the capacity to make his own decisions again, it was agreed I would no longer have to use the power of attorney or sign on Bob's behalf for any further procedures. Bob was able to express his own wishes now and, after discussing it with him and the doctors, we now felt it was the right time to remove the DNR instruction from his notes.

Wednesday [04/12/2019]

Sue: *Bob had a good and comfortable night. He is now sitting in a specialist chair and is communicating well. He is more comfortable with the tracheostomy. Things are improving daily. I'm sure he is ready for more visits and would like to see more people.*

Lauren: *That's amazing! We can't wait to see him Saturday. XX*

Charlie: *Amazing xx*

Emma: *Can't wait to see him Sunday and see the improvement. x*

Totty: *That is amazing!!! Go Bob x.*

Clive: *Our God raised him from the dead to a chair in a couple of weeks next stop Christmas then a speech at Emma's wedding.*

Thursday [05/12/2019]

Sue: *Rang the hospital, Bob is doing good, a peaceful night and in chair soon ready for physio. x*

Cheryl: *Good news Sue xxxx love you Sis. x*

Pat: *So many calls every day at the office Sue, all asking after Bob and wishing him well. x*

Clive: *Bob was good and he's so much better. I read Bob the list of who is on Team Bob and he showed interest. Me being me, I paired up wrong people and he soon put me right, so his brain is working ok. He moved his hands and feet a lot. He is now sleeping. I thank God for my friend Bob and my adopted Bloomfield family, Love you all. x*

Friday [06/12/2019]

Mike: *Just back from seeing Dad, all is good. He was tired but stayed awake for me. I can't be sure, but I think he tried to mime something with his mouth but obviously no air is there because of the tubes. When I asked if he was trying to talk, he kind of nodded.*

Saturday [07/12/2019]

Lisa: *Got a big thumbs up as we arrived, and he mouthed hello. We have had lots of chats with him, which he responded by thumbs up and wiggles of the feet. His squeezes are getting* stronger with both hands. We have had lots of smiles too as we laughed and remembered funny stories. He raised his hand to give us a big wave goodbye.

Pete: *Such an improvement from our visit last week - he's more focussed and understands all that we are saying and sharing with him. We can see the expressions in his eye/s and face - it's lovely to see. xx*

Powelly: *Superb news. What a man, with unbelievable strength and desire to push himself to get well again. Keep it up Bob.*

Jim: *Just seen Dad. Nurse said he was in chair for 2 hours but was feeling tired so was put back in bed. After he woke up, he wiggled his feet continuously the whole time we were there. He also lifted his right leg. He made a few smirks when me and Lauren were joking with him. When we told him that he was beating us on Super 6, he used his right hand to imitate cheering. The nurse said that he will be moving to a new ward very soon, possibly tomorrow or early next week as he doesn't need machines any more or critical/intensive care. He's no longer on the ventilator, they are just putting it on every 4 hours to check all his vitals then turning it off. x*

Sunday [08/12/2019]

Flis & Smithy: *An amazing uplifting visit with Bob today. He's quite tired as the ward had a few admissions last night, which disturbed his sleep. Generally, he's getting stronger even wanted to hold Kev the Carrot that we gave him. X*

Julie: *Just left Robert clutching his carrot!! He managed to keep his eyes open and conveyed to me that he was hot, so I fanned him with a piece of card which got a thumbs up!*

Monday [09/12/2019]

Emma: *Right, we have amazing news today. So, Dad's sense of humour is still there, I said I love you to him, he mouthed back 'love me to' which he always says to me! Then he smiled and laughed. They had tried him with a speaking value before we arrived, but his breath rates weren't very good, so they had to put him back on the oxygen. They tried again while we were here, it's hard to hear him as its very weak, but he said, 'I love Emma.' He also said something that we couldn't work out because it's very hard to understand him at the moment. But we used an alphabet chart that the speech and language therapist left with him to get the first letter of the words. We got him to squeeze our hand when we pointed to a letter that was right until it spelt out a word and then we worked out what he was saying 'I don't like the chair' which is the one they put him in sometimes. So that means he can remember how to spell as well. But big news is... they have just moved him to a new ward, and we helped him to settle in. He is on Sahara B Bay 2. It is still two to a bed and visiting is 10.30am till 7.30pm. When you come in go up the stairs and follow it round all the way to the orange lift. It is on the second floor x.*

Flis & Smithy: *What amazing news. Quite remarkable well-done Bob!!!*

Heidi: *Absolutely wonderful updates. Sending so much love xxxx*

Sue: *It's so good to see Bob doing so well. I feel so elated and over the moon.*

Claire & Andy: *Wow what a wonderful day it has been. Bob's story never ceases to amaze us.*

Tuesday [10/12/2019]

Jim: *Dad had a good first night on the new ward and slept through most of it.*

Julie: *Robert looks so much better today. Much more responsive the best I have seen him. They are going to switch the tracheostomy off twice a day for 30 mins to get him used to breathing through his mouth. He is in a nice bay of four beds.*

Wednesday [11/12/2019]

Wiggy: *Spent a good 45 minutes with Bob today. He was far more responsive with thumbs up a few times. I had good chat with the nurse, and they are waiting for the referral to move him to Colchester. Once referred they have to wait for a bed to be available.*

Flis & Smithy: *Colchester Stroke Unit is amazing, it's one of the best. It's also good that Bob will be closer to home for the family to make regular visits to Bob, we as friends can also pop in much more regularly. I'm so flabbergasted Bob is doing so incredibly well. Dead proud of the family too. Xxx Very honoured to have you all in our lives.*

Thursday [12/12/2019]

Emma: *Just spoke to Mum. She has been to see Dad today he was very tired, but it could be because they are working him hard. The nurse told her that they don't have to suction his tracheostomy anymore which means he is swallowing a bit more now. The one he has in at the moment is a size 8 and they want to get him to a size 6 but they don't think he needs it anymore. So, they are going to try taking the tracheostomy out (probably not this week though) and let it close up and see how he gets on. This also means he will be able to try and talk a bit more and might not be so hard.*

Mum washed his face today and was able to brush his teeth which probably made him feel a bit better. He is doing so well x.

Friday [13/12/2019]

Mike: *We put some music on for Dad and he was showing us some dance moves with his feet. Looks like they will put the speaking valve in for most of the day on Monday, that's good as it's only been in for half an hour at a time before. x*

Saturday [14/12/2019]

Jim: *Dad is more tired at the moment as he may have a chest infection, he is already on antibiotics just in case. They are not putting the speaking valve on until the infection has gone. We asked the nurse to write on his board that he likes his feet uncovered as he gets hot easily. We also restocked his shower gel.*

Liz: *He has done so well. Miracles do happen x.*

Sunday [15/12/2019]

Emma: *Dad is starting to move his left foot a little bit more now. I asked if he wanted me to wash his face and he squeezed my hand, so I did with a cold flannel. I also took the sheet off as he was hot. I asked if that was better, he nodded. He knows Mum is coming up tomorrow and gave a little smile x. As we left, I asked him to show us his wave, he got his right arm all the way up and waved really well.*

Monday [16/12/2019]

Sue: *Bob had the voice valve in today and the timescale was increased to an hour. His sats remained very good while he tried to talk. He said a couple of words and with the help of the alphabet* *chart, we were able to understand what he was saying. He had to be reminded to raise eyebrows for no and to blink hard for yes, so may need clarity and reminding when people visit him. But I think it depends on how tired he is at the time. He's in good spirits. X*

Tuesday [17/12/2019]

Jim: *Called hospital about Christmas Day visits and we can visit from 9am. It's slightly more lenient but no guarantees they'll allow more than two people at a time. Also, Dad's been accepted on waiting list for Colchester, could be before Christmas, could be after x.*

Mike: *Dad seemed to move lots more than usual today. He was yawning and had an itch on his chest which he managed to scratch. He moved his left arm up a bit which he hasn't really done before. His speech valve was in and he was trying hard to talk. We had to step outside the bay while the nurse checked his stats and made him comfortable. Once he was refreshed and all ready, we tried listening again to see if we could hear him, but he didn't talk, then we found out they'd taken the voice valve out, but we didn't know and Dad couldn't tell us! lol. With hand signals Dad said they've put a smaller size tube in and then acted like he was holding a glass and drinking indicating he was thirsty. He's not allowed to drink yet in case he swallows wrong as he could choke, which might cause infection, but the nurse got a wet gauze on a stick and moistened his lips and Dad was able to suck the water from it. We're allowed to offer this to him, but we must hold it, so he doesn't choke if we do it with him.*

Wednesday [18/12/2019]

Julie: *A positive visit. So much more alert than Sunday. Robert was in the specialist chair and his voice valve was in. Nurse explained when valve is in, he's breathing normally, they'll increase* the time he has this in so eventually he won't need tracheostomy. Apparently, he's tolerating this very well, a lot of patients don't. He's also swallowing to clear his throat most of the time which is a good sign. His blood pressure is now normal. Bought him a handheld fan which definitely got a thumbs up, he was able to hold it himself for a little while.

Thursday [19/12/2019]

Wiggy: *Bob was pretty good today. I told him all about my boy Joe's birthday etc and he was definitely listening. He raised his right hand as I left, so I held it and he squeezed. As I left the nurse saw what happened and said he tried to say something to me. Absolutely brilliant and made me fill up whilst going back to the car.*

Cheryl: *Bob is good doing well. Physio very pleased with him. I did notice his eye was red, so they are going to get the doctor to check it as he said it was sore.*

Friday [20/12/2019]

Sue: *Bob has had physio today; I spoke to consultant and he said Bob is doing well and things have turned around and moving forward. He never expected this outcome and so quick! Bob will need a lot of rehab and they will introduce different types of rehab to support Bob's needs. The speech valve has been stepped up to 2 hours and Bob is coping well. He enjoyed the hand massage and foot massage so anyone who feels comfortable to do that for him please do. We ask him first and if you get thumbs up, he means yes. Some of his work colleagues visited him today as well. All in all, things are very good, and I want to say thank you so much to all my wonderful family and special friends because without all your love and support for both Bob and me things could have been very different, I love you all and am so grateful to have the* *wonderful network that we share. keep it going for by doing so, you are helping Bob in his recovery x.*

Maxine: *I'm so glad xx*

Rab: *Great news I am dumbfound by the turnaround a proper Christmas miracle.*

Cheryl: *I was with Sue today. We need to keep Bob positive ask him to lift his legs and move himself arms if he can. We need to keep him strong both mentally and physically and focus on how well he is doing. It must be hard on him not being able to do what he is used to at the moment. So, keep his spirits up.*

Clive: *I cannot thank everyone enough for all the updates on Bob. I am now in Thailand until 17 January, but my prayers will be with him every day. God has given Bob life and now I pray that God will give life to him more abundantly, so he is back to playing golf and enjoying partying with all his wonderful friends. To God be the glory great things he hath done. May the grace of our Lord Jesus Christ be with you now and forever. All my love Clive*

Saturday [21/12/2019]

Gwen: *It was good to see Bob today. He was clearly tired & kept shutting his eyes but listened to and acknowledged what I was saying to him. He raised his left arm when the nurse asked him to and constantly moved his toes & right hand. I'm sure all our visits are helping & giving him encouragement xx*

Jim: *The nurse said Dad asked to go in the chair today. He was in there for over 2 hours. He indicated that he was uncomfortable and tried to mouth this to us soon after we arrived - so was put back in the bed. He seemed happy and was smirking and he stayed* *awake for the whole visit. He moved his left arm slightly off the bed and squeezed our hands with his left. He moves his right arm a lot more now, he was hot and took the bed sheet off himself. As we left, he did a massive wave with a raised arm and was still smiling and dancing with his feet to fairy tale of New York x.*

Sunday [22/12/2019] One month after responding from coma.

Pete & Lisa: *Bob was sitting in his chair and gave us a big wave as we walked in before we even spoke to him. I asked if he wanted his feet massaged to which I got a thumbs up. So, he had a 20 minute pamper session. Having not been for 2 weeks we can definitely see the difference in the movement on his left side. He was enjoying the Christmas songs tapping away most of the visit.*

Bob was doing so well that the doctors decided it was time to refer him to a specialist hospital for intensive rehabilitation, which would help his recovery even further. A referral to Queen's Square London NHNN and Northwick Park Regional Rehab Unit was sent. However, we were told the waiting lists could be up to two months. In the meantime, we would just have to wait for a bed to become available at Colchester, so Bob could continue his rehab there and he would also be closer to home.

Wednesday [25/12/2019] Christmas Day

Powelly: *Merry Christmas Bob.*

Jim: *Thanks mate I'll pass it on. He has been in very good spirits this morning. He moved both arms and legs. We have done secret Santa and got lots of smiles from him. He is pointing with both hands and chose who was going to open their presents next. Merry Christmas everyone and I'll pass on your well wishes to Dad x.*

Christmas has always been a special time of year for our family to get together, although some traditions had changed slightly over the years. Since our children were now adults and living in homes of their own, they had decided that it would be better for them as siblings to skip buying individual gifts and adopt a Secret Santa style of gifting. Although we continued giving the children individual gifts, Bob and I also joined in with the Secret Santa gift idea. It proved to be great fun. This year, just like other years, at the beginning of November, names were pulled out of the hat, a spending limit of £25 per person had been set and £5 of that budget had to include a jokey type of present.

On the morning of Christmas Day, the children and partners all came over to mine to spend the day and we all travelled to see Bob at the hospital. With our sack full of Secret Santa gifts, we made our way to the ward and greeted the staff with a 'Merry Christmas' and a box of chocolates. I had previously told the kids I wasn't going to ask the nurses if we could all go in together as I didn't want to highlight the two to a bed rule. I had a feeling if we just all walked up to Bob's bed, the staff would be unlikely to say anything especially as it was Christmas Day, so that's exactly what we did!

The Team Bob WhatsApp group was inundated with Christmas wishes for Bob and after big hugs all round, the Secret Santa unwrapping commenced. Before we opened our gifts, I asked Bob if he had remembered who his Secret Santa was and what he had bought them as these had been purchased before Bob had fallen ill with his stroke. Bob nodded his head indicating yes and did a thumbs up with a smile.

One by one, Bob chose who would open their presents next and left Will until last. As Will opened his parcel, we could see a lovely royal blue Hugo Boss top, he then proceeded to unwrap the next gift, we all laughed as he pulled out a child's musical bath toy set. Needless to say, I think this gave the game away and we all knew who Will's secret Santa was!

I have such fond memories of that day: my family was around me, we were all of us so happy, and my husband was improving day by day, which was the best gift ever. While I have been writing this book, Bob has also told me that this is his first clear memory of what happened after he woke up from the coma.

Thursday [26/12/2019] Boxing Day

Julie: *Mum and Dad have been today. They hadn't been able to see Robert for a week due to colds, they couldn't believe the improvement in him. He could clearly understand what Mum and Dad were saying to him and reacted accordingly with his feet! They used the fan to cool him and massaged his hands. They both said it was the best he has been, and I think it made their Christmas xx*

Friday [27/12/2019]

Emma: *The doctors wanted to check inside Dad's throat and used a camera to investigate and take a look at his windpipe. They said the majority of the swelling has gone down, but the throat is still a little swollen. They gave him some water and yoghurt to swallow while the camera was there and a little bit of it does go down the wrong tube. They are going to give him a little bit of water once a day to get his muscles working as they are weak in that area. But they are now going to keep the speaking value in for 12 hours a day and only take it off at night. They said it is all positive but can't be sure if the fluid going down the wrong way is from any damage caused by the stroke or the swelling so only time will tell that one. Also, Dad said to me that he was fed up which I said I know but every time I come you are a lot better and able to do more. I told him he has to work hard to help improve himself and that he has the wedding to work for. Then I said will you do it for me Dad and he nodded yes. x*

Saturday [28/12/2019]

Rab: *So amazed walked in to see Bob and he mouthed Rab and put his hand out to shake, I am so impressed with how far he has come and today he seemed positive and looked good, he rolled his eyes when I said if his hair kept growing, he'd have more than me!*

Wiggy: *I've just got back and what a massive improvement. He lifted his left arm, which I've not seen before. Also muttered getting better. The nurse said he is doing brilliant and now needs to go to rehab. Absolutely amazing visit.*

Cheryl: *All good very much alert today. Bob needs a desk fan if someone has one, can they bring it in as a matter of urgency. I explained to him how well he has done and how far he has come. And he must not give up. Rehab will be hard but lots of people like him do a great recovery. And he must move his body as much as he can.*

Sunday [29/12/2019]

Flis & Smithy: *So pleased to see a HUGE difference. He was "chatting" initially wanting to know where we'd been!! But rapidly became tired. Dead chuffed to see Bob and his progress.*

Lisa: *Sue, Lisa and Pete reporting, Bob was able to hold the gel stress balls in both hands today, he transferred them from his right to his left and then back again. We didn't ask him to do this, he knew what he wanted to do. We've shared lots of chats, laughter, smiles, and love today. He is feeling a bit fed up, but Bob has always been active with his mind and body, so this is a normal reaction and a good sign. We've told him how well he's doing and how proud all of Team Bob are of him. He was tired and so was transferred from the chair back into his bed. Such a big change since we were with him last Sunday - he's a Superstar.*

Monday [30/12/2019]

Emma: *Dad looks good today! His speech is getting stronger, the nurse said she hasn't seen him for a few days and thinks he looks so much better. He's tired but is communicating well. He did say 'what am I doing today' meaning he wanted to do some sort of physio. They said he is on the physio list, and they want to see him today or tomorrow. The speech and language have tried Dad again with 4 teaspoons of water, he got tired, and it was slower swallowing but they are very pleased with him and are going to discuss with the doctors about taking the tracheostomy out today or tomorrow. Dad said he wants his phone so I'm going to take it to Nana and Grandads later and if Julie, you can bring it with you tomorrow.*

Tuesday [31/12/2019] New Year's Eve

Emma: *Can you put Wills parents down for Saturday afternoon to see Dad please Julie. x*

Julie: *Good news Robert's tracheostomy has been removed. The nurse said that now the tracheostomy is out there's a greater chance of him being transferred to Colchester as he will not need a critical care bed. He now has his phone, so u can send messages, if you visit can u see if he has any and read them to him. He didn't want me to put the phone on the table when we left, he wanted to hold it. When u visit can u make sure it doesn't need charging. He is allowed calls but at the moment someone will have to be there to help him. Cheryl and Rab phoned him, and I put it on loudspeaker so he could hear. Happy new year to you all. Xx*

It was New Year's Eve, and all was well. Everyone could enjoy the celebrations knowing that Bob was doing so well. Claire and Andy had kindly invited me over to there's and Emma and Will offered to drive me. It was a lovely gesture, but I decided that I would have a quiet night in. I knew there would be local fireworks and how unsettled these make Archie, so I didn't want to leave the dogs alone. As I settled in for the night, I ordered a takeaway, opened a bottle of red, put the television on high volume to mask some of the firework noise, and snuggled up on the sofa with the dogs.

2020 was imminent and I was ready!..................

Chapter Eight:

Steppingstones to Milestones

I welcomed the new year with much optimism. Bob was improving daily, achieving incredible results. On January 4th, he was transferred to a lower dependency unit. Whilst there, he continued to work hard with many different types of therapists. It wasn't long before Bob took part in physio twice a day! I recall how they had helped him to sit up on the edge of the bed and, using a specialist piece of equipment called a 'return,' they even managed to get Bob to a standing position for a few seconds.

We were aware that the part of the brain affected (the cerebellum) controlled balance and I remember Emma asking me soon after her dad woke up from the coma if I thought he would be able to walk her down the aisle. That was always the one question everyone wanted to know: 'would Bob be able to walk again?' Every time someone asked this question, whether it was directed at me or not, my reply always remained the same: "Absolutely, I know he will!" and I never lost sight of that!

Although Bob had lost a lot of weight and muscle tone, and the feeding tube was still attached to his stomach via his nose, the hole where his tracheostomy had been started to close up and heal. You could see he was beginning to look a bit more like his old self. Bob was spending more time in the chair and Emma was finally able to give her dad a much-needed haircut. It was definitely a talking point because, as Bob's hair kept growing, it seemed to defy the law of gravity; no matter how long it got, it continued to point upwards!

On 9th January, Bob was repatriated back to the Colchester Hospital Stroke Unit. I remember waiting outside his room on Acute One Ward as the nurses helped Bob into his bed. To start with, Bob had to be hoisted in and out of the bed while they changed his bedding or transferred him into the specialist chair. The staff had remembered Bob from his critical moment back in November, they were so kind and very helpful. They told me I was welcome to stay with Bob to help settle him in and said to call them if there was anything we needed. The room was quite spacious; however, the furniture was situated to Bob's left and I could tell its current layout would not work for him. I decided to rearrange the furniture to make things more accessible. Once the bedside cabinet and table had been moved to his right-hand side, he could reach for his glasses, iPad, and iPhone. I also put the fan on the table so he would be able to turn this on or off himself; it was important for Bob to feel empowered and I knew this would definitely help him with his recovery.

I was sure wearing his own clothes would also make him feel a little better, so I had brought some of them in. They were summer clothes, so I thought they would also help him stay cooler on the unit. He watched as I unpacked his shorts and t-shirts. Some of his tops buttoned up around the neckline. I had specifically chosen these as I thought they would be easier for the nurses to dress Bob since they went over his head and would help to avoid any pressure on the scar tissue.

A nurse had said that we could place some photos of family and friends in his room on the wall for Bob to look at. It was a brilliant idea and enabled Bob to feel more at home. It also sparked conversation, as staff and visitors would ask Bob who the people were in the photos. This was a fantastic way to encourage Bob to talk more. Of course, Archie and Honey were also part of the picture collage.

After everything had been set up in his room, I stayed a little longer until it was time to go. I told Bob to get some sleep, as I knew he would be very busy doing rehabilitation exercises tomorrow. Before I left, I gave Bob a hug and a kiss and placed the alarm call button to his right-hand side and told him I would be back in the morning, he responded with a thumbs up.

The following day, I was pleased to see that the nurses had dressed Bob in his shorts and t-shirt. He looked really good! He wanted to show me how he had been practicing writing my name with a special pen; writing became another method to communicate and clarify things if his speech wasn't clear. It also helped his brain to relearn the fine motor skills that had been lost by his stroke.

It wasn't long before the physiotherapists and occupational therapists arrived. There were so many nurses and staff who worked with Bob, but I particularly remember Ellie, Emma, Nic, Lucy, and Laura as they worked with Bob quite regularly. They certainly gave him no time to slack and started rehabilitation straight away. I watched as they brought the 'return' equipment into the room and two of them attempted to get Bob to sit up on the side of the bed while supporting his torso. It was hoped that, by doing these different exercises, in time Bob would start to regain control over his balance and develop his core strength.

To start with, the therapists did most of Bob's rehabilitation exercises on the bed in his room, where he was helped to move into a seated position and then supported to stand for a few seconds. Then other exercises were introduced to help his limb movements and also hand and eye coordination. By repeating these exercises, his brain perceived the need for a function and started to rewire accordingly, creating a bridge from steppingstones to milestones.

While Bob remained at Colchester, friends and family continued to visit him and everyone continued interaction and support. I remember how Pete encouraged Bob to use the electric shaver, helping him by guiding his hand. It didn't take long before Bob took over and started to shave himself, he was so determined.

On 14th January, the family attended a meeting with medical professionals. I was hoping that Dr El-rekaby would be there, however, it was a different doctor coordinating Bob's care on that day. After the initial introductions, and a recap on Bob's stroke, they explained that they didn't want to keep the feed tube in his nose for too much longer to enable their speech and language team to continue working with Bob. With their help, it was hoped that Bob would soon be able to manage fluid and food intake in the normal way.

They wanted to get to know a bit more about him and started to ask us questions about his family network, occupation, interests, and hobbies, as this would help them to create a person-centred plan around his rehab, referral, and recovery program.

"Does Bob have any goals you think he would be keen to work towards?" the consultant asked.

Emma replied, "I'm due to get married in May and obviously Dad was going to walk me down the aisle, do you think this will be possible within the time limit?"

The consultant replied, "The type of stroke your dad suffered is so rare that unfortunately there isn't much data on outcomes, so I am unable to say whether your dad will walk again in time for your wedding day. However, our physio and occupational teams will certainly work with him to give him every chance until a place becomes available at one of the intensive rehab hospitals."

Again, I wanted to reassure Emma, "I believe your dad will be able to walk you down the aisle Emma, I know he will!" I could tell some people thought my optimism may have been set too high, but I was adamant that Bob would be walking our daughter down the aisle. Yes, I knew we had a long road ahead, the wedding was just under five months away and I knew it would take much work, however, Bob had already shown such great strength, courage, and determination. To walk our daughter down the aisle would be the ultimate goal and to read his father of the bride speech would also be a great incentive to work towards.

We agreed a referral to the Regional Hyper-acute Rehabilitation Unit Northwick Park Hospital Harrow was the way forward although it would mean Bob would not be so close to home anymore; it was the best place to receive rehabilitation at the intense level he required. In the meantime, Bob would continue his rehabilitation at Colchester. I thanked the medical team for their support and went to see Bob to explain the plan.

The team at Colchester continued to support Bob and it wasn't long before he progressed to the gym which was situated in the unit. It had various pieces of equipment such as walking bars, benches, mock stairs, and all kinds of gym exercise balls to help with coordination and core balance. In addition, they ran various groups including music, quizzes, and games.

Wednesday [15/01/2020]

Julie: *Mum and Dad visited this morning just as they were taking Robert to a music group session. It was the first time he had been out of his room. He was seated in his specialist chair. Robert had to swing his arms in time to music, then clap and make hand movements. He was given a musical instrument (bells) and sang along to 'We'll Meet Again' (just his era!) They passed a ball around with questions on it, when it stopped at Robert, his question was favourite take away, he answered Chinese, Mum said he spoke so clear. My parents felt it was a rewarding visit and nice to see the therapy in action.*

Sue: *Bob went to the Gym this afternoon for physiotherapy. They helped Bob to stand and then move to sit on a flat bed. He was able to support himself sitting up without being held by anyone.*

They got him to lift his right arm to assess his balance while sitting. He was able to raise his legs simultaneously and managed to hold his torso straight and kept his head high without losing his strength and balance on his upper body. The therapist will work with Bob daily. A good visit and again, heart-warming to see. We have now completed the hand and arm exercises that the physio has left for us to do. Copy of these on Bob's table, please feel free to do these with Bob when you visit, it all helps.

Emma: *I spoke to Dad on the phone when Mum was there and that was the clearest I heard him talk and that was over the phone!*

Bob was smashing the boundaries every day; his muscle strength and limb movements were increasing as he continued to work hard with all the therapists. The nurses on the ward also provided great care. Understandably, there were a few hiccups along the way. He picked up the odd chest infection and urinary tract infection, but the medical teams were quick to treat these.

He was also getting used to sitting and standing for longer periods of time and his brain was trying to adapt to this sensation after laying down in a horizontal position for a long time whilst in the coma and in the early days of recovering. This meant sometimes the sensation of being upright, as well as working hard on therapy exercises, made Bob feel dizzy and sick as his body adjusted, so he was prescribed anti sickness drugs to counteract this which really helped.

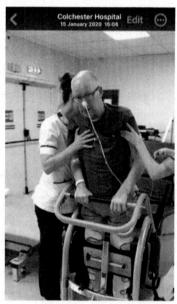

I visited Bob every day and, for

the majority of the time, I accompanied Bob in his physio sessions. I could see this was very tiring for him, but he was doing so well and just kept going. I kept a video diary of some of the exercises which were really useful for Bob to see. By doing so, he was able to see for himself how much he was improving. It gave him the encouragement to keep 'moving forward'. I shared the videos on Team Bob too; the progress he was making was so incredible that everyone was amazed as they watched them.

Now Bob was closer to home, he could receive even more visits from our extended families. I recall seeing my sister Allie a few times as she had popped in to see Bob whilst she was there also visiting other people. I often saw aunties and uncles on both sides of our families who made great efforts to visit Bob many times. Plus some of his work colleagues, old and new and many more of our friends and neighbours, and my TAG family too. TAG is the affectionate name for a dog agility club where I trained with Archie and Honey. Cheryl is a member too.

We have a lovely circle of friends there. Sal, Max, Ellie, Jackie, and Gloria were so supportive. Sal didn't live far from the hospital and was so kind inviting me over for meals each week, as she knew I'd been at the hospital all day. Jackie visited Bob a number of times with Cheryl. Max also visited with her daughter Ellie. Max and Cheryl often met me at home, sometimes after work, and we would walk the dogs together and talk things through. Gloria often texted me sending so much love to us all. It was lovely to have people who reached out to me and offered their support. But there were two more very eager and special visitors yet to see Bob... Archie and Honey were a big part of Bob's recovery plan and a visit was arranged for them to see their 'Daddy.'

On Sunday 19th January Emma and I arrived at the Stroke Unit and waited with Honey and Archie in the communal room. I truly believe they knew what was about to happen. As soon as the double doors began to open, Honey and Archie could see their dad being pushed towards them in his chair. They were so excited as he approached but sensed they had to be gentle. They could also smell the dog treats I had placed in Bob's hand for him to give to them. Archie was quite vocal, barking with excitement. Bob started to stroke him with his right hand trying to say 'shush.' This was good as it encouraged Bob to move his arm and speak at the same time. Honey was thrilled to see Bob and stood on her back legs placing her front paws on the arms of his chair to get closer. It was so lovely to see their reunion and it brought tears to my eyes. We videoed this special moment and shared it with 'Team Bob'. It was a massive boost for Bob and everyone. While Bob remained at Colchester, Honey and Archie remained regular visitors to the ward.

Sunday [19/01/2020]

Maxine: *Ah that is so lovely brought a tear to my eyes, Bob is looking so much brighter and has come on so well, the dogs were so gentle (mind you thought Archie would be) xx*

Sal: *So lovely to see! Come on Bob! You are doing so well x.*

Jackie: *It was so moving to see Archie and Honey with Bob xxx*

Wiggy: *Oh, Sue that one made me cry, with joy though. Wiggy x*

Cheryl: *Wow lovely to see the dogs with Bob he is doing so well, Keep going Bob. X*

The specialist chair was also used to take Bob to the gym. The nurses would help him transfer from this onto the apparatus or couch. Bob was encouraged to sit up on the couch to help strengthen his core and torso. They would then give Bob a balloon to throw to them while he was seated, which eventually turned into a game of catch. He was also supported into the standing position and would hold on to the bars, helping him to get used to balancing. He was a bit wobbly at first, but they had a tall standing mirror so Bob could see himself and this somehow seemed to help him balance better. Watching Bob achieve so much was very heart-warming. My eyes would often leak tears of joy as it was so incredible to witness.

As Bob's muscle mass began to increase, he soon mastered standing whilst holding onto the support bars. He was soon introduced to the walking bars and his brain was quick to learn. I could see he found it hard to move his legs forward at first and it was very tiring for him, but he persevered through it all. The time came when Bob didn't need the specialist chair anymore; incredibly, he could sit in a normal style wheelchair and use his hands and arms to push himself while moving his legs in a walking motion to propel the chair forward.

   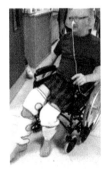

On Saturday 25th January, Bob was moved onto Block C which was a four-bay unit almost opposite where he had been before. This was good because he now had company with three fellow patients and I felt that this would stimulate him to do even more.

On the Stroke Unit, they also ran a peer support group for family and friends to get together and share experiences and ideas. This was held every Friday in the communal room. It was helpful to be able to talk to others in a similar situation. We all looked out for each other and the patients on the ward. One day before I had arrived, Bob had been sick. A lovely lady called Sandra was visiting her husband, Les, and she saw Bob needed help, so she called for the nurse. It was very comforting to know that we had a helping hand between peers. Les also loved visits from Archie and Honey.

Bob continued to surprise us all by achieving extraordinary results and, as usual whenever he passed from a steppingstone to a milestone, it was always shared in 'Team Bob'. Messages of love, encouragement and support for Bob would come flooding in. I feel it's important I acknowledge these and continue to give these a special place in the book, exactly as they were written at the time. Not only do they capture and give a true reflection of Bob's amazing achievements, but they also express the feelings and personal experiences of all those who witnessed such incredible and sometimes unexpected results.

Saturday [25/01/2020]

Jim: *This morning, I was very surprised to see I had a text from Dad. He tried to text me to say he had moved. He must have known we were coming. Although the message wasn't typed correctly it was great that he tried. When we saw him, he was quite chatty and doing loads of things for himself. We can definitely see a massive improvement; he was picking up things for himself and speaking answers rather than giving thumbs up. All his family photos were up on his new wall as well.*

Monday [27/01/2020]

Emma: *In physio he managed with their help to get from the bed to his bedside chair with no return aid. He was on the edge of the bed standing up and shuffled over to the chair! The physio just came to speak to us and told us she recorded him! She was very pleased with him!*

Wednesday [29/01/2020]

Sue: *The OT Emma has said that Bob had a shower with their support and although mostly sitting down on a chair aid, he was standing a few seconds holding on to a rail. He has also just had the speech and language therapist here and Bob fed himself with 4 teaspoons of yogurt and the therapist gave him 3 teaspoons of water under supervision. Bob did well with no problems.*

Time was going so quickly now in comparison to those sad days back in November. It was now February and things were looking so much brighter for everyone. As I entered the ward on a chilly February morning, Dr El-rekaby saw me and said he would come over shortly to discuss the latest MRI results from the scan Bob had had the week before. After about ten minutes he arrived at the bay and began to explain the results to us both. He wanted to reassure us the scan had shown no damage to the brain stem. The only part of the brain affected was the left half of the cerebellum. Dr El-rekaby told us it may be possible to make a full recovery with time, hard work, and intense rehab. He said it could take up to six months or a year to reach full recovery although there could be some lingering balance issues but only time would tell.

Because Bob was younger than a person normally affected by a stroke this had advantages for his recovery. With Bob's determination and everyone's continued love and support, the prognosis was good. It was just magic to see the smile on Bob's face when he was shown the images and told that recovery was possible. Again, we shared this good news with all of 'Team Bob'. As soon as I posted the news, this was the response…

Monday [03/02/2020]

Charlie: *Amazing! xx*

Lauren: *Brilliant news x*

Simon: *Come on Bob!!*

Gwen: *That is brilliant news xx*

Totty: *Go Bob and all the team*

Kim: *A miracle God bless you all how amazing.*

Sal: *Fantastic news!* 🙏😇🏃 *Archie knows!*

Jackie: *Fabulous news, Bob your Amazing, the determination to get better shows in the improvement you achieve every day xx*

Maxine: *Amen* 🙏 *this is such great news and now I think Archie is telling us that dad don't need that tube after he sat on it and accidently pulled it out!*

Meeli: *Such amazing news! Mum, Darren, Coops, and I are all sending our love and we are so thrilled to hear just how incredibly Bob is doing!*

Flis & Smithy: *Sue I can't explain how wonderful this news is to read! Absolutely marvellous news for you all. I'll sort out a day to come up I'll let Julie know, much love* 🖤

Clive: *Absolutely, stay strong, don't give up.*

Tuesday [04/02/2020]

Mike: *Had a good meeting with doctors and therapist about Dad. They reiterated that his brain stem has no damage at all. His cerebellum is damaged, and this is the bit that controls balance but also fine tunes most things the brain does. So fine tuning his movement etc. However, they said that the possibility is there to relearn this. They are confident he will make at least an 80% recovery but couldn't give us any specifics on walking as his case is so rare. They are pleased with his progress as a whole but want to keep pushing him for things like talking and swallowing. But are conscious not to over push him as this might actually set him back.*

Bob continued to be tube fed, but this was slowly being reduced as he was working with the therapist on food trials (level 5). This included eating things like mashed-up banana, shepherd's pie, and curry made from mince. Eventually he was up to three trial meals a day and was also allowed to drink a few teaspoonfuls of his favourite Tetley tea!

Monday [10/02/2020]

Emma: *Just went to see Dad he has just finishing a physio session! He did really well at that and did a bit of walking with the rails. Dad was able to walk about 20 steps from the gym out to corridor with the support of four members of staff. His energy levels are so much better as he is tired but not exhausted. Mum got him to write, and his writing is a lot better, really neat and in the lines! He had a pamper and we have just left him to rest while we get some lunch.*

UPDATE: We went with Dad to the dining room; he had chicken curry (Level 5) which he loved! He's also got some strawberry mousse for later tonight! Also had a cup of tea fed to him! He did have an extra teaspoon of curry 😊 He was fine with all this no problems! Then the physio asked if he wanted to take himself back to his bay! Mum video it! He can push himself along in his wheelchair to get himself back to his bed! Then they helped him back to bed! It was a really good visit xx

Bob's birthday was fast approaching; it was only two days away and his wish was to be able to have his favourite dessert, which was jelly and ice cream!

Tuesday [11/02/2020]

Jim: *We have just left Dad. Went to visit as Lauren is working tomorrow. He was awake and on his phone when we arrived. Gave him some presents and a balloon with which he was pleased. He made a few jokes. We have left him to sleep as he has had a busy day. He was in good spirits and looking forward to more family time on his birthday tomorrow. But more importantly* *looking forward to that jelly and ice cream* 😋 *x*

Bob had set himself another goal to work for and he absolutely smashed it!

Happy Birthday Bob!

Wednesday [12/02/2020]

Simon: *Bob, many happy returns, and best wishes on your birthday. You're an amazing guy!*

Julie: *Visited Robert with Mum and Dad. He opened his cards and presents by himself and laughed at my T-shirt slogan.*

Sal: *I love this x.*

Maxine: *Love this hope you enjoyed your ice cream Bob x.*

Jackie: *The change in Bob each day is a miracle, this picture is* *amazing Bob looks so good. Hope u enjoyed your jelly & ice cream.*

Thursday [13/02/2020]

Sue: *Nurses said Bob is doing well and also said they have spoken to the Specialty Stroke Doctor throughout this whole journey, who has also said it's a miracle!*

Cheryl: *Double on way home xx was thinking about Bob!*

Thursday [20/02/2020]

Gwen: *It was so lovely to see Bob. The progress he has made since I last saw him is amazing. He has a sparkle in his eyes & he reminded me what a wicked sense of humour he has. Bob was on good form, laughing at the boys' stories. They were pleased to have seen him & see just how much progress he is making. I thought his speech had improved. xx*

Bob continued to excel, and more good news followed; we were told Bob would soon be moving to Northwick Park Hospital to start the intensive rehabilitation program and, since he was doing so well and would soon be leaving Colchester Hospital, they decided that, once visiting hours had finished, they would move him to the Acute Two area. Bob said he would text to let me know which bay he was on. I did have to laugh when I received his text! For those reading this who don't already know him, it paints the perfect picture of his optimism, resilience, and brilliant sense of humour.

Bob: *I'm now on E Bay ………room 4 xx*

Sue: *Are you buy it now or do I have to bid xx*

Bob: No reserve, collection only xx

Chapter Nine:

Intensive Rehabilitation

It was agreed Bob would be transferred to the Regional Hyper-acute Rehabilitation Unit, Northwick Park Hospital, Harrow, (Flemming Ward) on Tuesday 25th February 2020 to start his intense rehabilitation program. As part of the plan, I was asked to attend a meeting at Northwick Park the day before he was admitted. Emma came with me. This gave us an opportunity to meet the medical team, discuss Bob's support plans and any goals that would help him in his recovery and also to see the ward and facilities where he would be spending the next three months.

It was a busy Monday morning as Emma and I began our journey to Northwick Park hospital and it took us about one hour forty-five minutes to arrive. Once there, we parked up in their multi-story car park and bought a ticket which was a similar price to Colchester, then made our way into the hospital building. The actual hospital looked very old and in need of some modernisation, but, as they say, you should never judge a book by its cover! We made our way into the main entrance following the tired corridors past the fruit stall, shops, and cafes until we reached the lifts at the end of the corridor. Flemming Ward was on Level 6, so we took the lift to the sixth floor and as we walked out of the lift, the Flemming Ward was literally just on the right.

To gain entrance to the ward, we had to buzz the intercom and explained we were there for a meeting about Bob. A nurse came to the door and we were taken to a room to meet the team. The staff were all very nice and once they explained how it all worked, we were then shown around the unit to see the distinct types of rehabilitation zones. These included the gym and occupational therapy areas, such as the kitchen area, community room and utility areas to help rehabilitation with washing, laundry, and meal preparation. However, to start with, most of Bob's time would be spent in the gym until he was ready for the next stage.

They explained the first two weeks would be a bit slow as the different types of therapists had to have all their meetings with Bob to get to know him first. They would need to find out more about him, including any goals Bob wanted to work on, for example walking and speech, which were both relevant to our daughter's forthcoming wedding. They would also chat with him to find out his hobbies and interests, using this to create a person-centred plan and coordinate his program. Review meetings with family to update on progress were scheduled for every six weeks. He would be given a weekly timetable: visiting times on the ward were 11.00am – 9.00pm and they only allow two visitors to the bedside. It would make sense to plan our visits to coincide with his free time and each other. If Bob was up to it, and for a change of scenery, we would be able to take him in the wheelchair to the ground floor of the hospital, where the café and shops were situated.

We were told that the normal length of stay was around two to three months, depending on the patient's needs. They tried to incorporate weekend home visits, so, it may be possible for Bob to come home on a Friday night and return to the hospital on the Sunday evening, depending of course on how well he improved over the next few weeks. They explained activities were reduced at weekends and it could feel a little boring for patients, so Saturdays and Sundays were a good time for visitors to see him.

It all sounded really good and we felt happy that Bob would be getting the next level of support. We had already told them that his dearest wish was to escort Emma down the aisle. We also explained he would want help with speech therapy to enable him to read his wedding speech. They thought the wedding goal was lovely and were very keen to help him to achieve his father of the bride duties. They said the incentive for Bob to do that would keep him focused. It was all so positive and as we left the hospital, Emma updated 'Team Bob.'

Monday [24/02/2020, 17:24:09]

Emma: *All good! And Dad's happy cause I told him they have a bath he can use 🛁 they will do a proper assessment of Dad when he gets there and will be able to give us better timeframes etc. She did say even if he is in hospital when the wedding happens, he will be allowed weekend release for it! Fingers crossed he is home by then, but we will see x*

On the morning of Tuesday 25th February, I went to see Bob at Colchester Hospital and waited with him for the hospital transport to arrive. It wasn't long before he was on his way. We said a grateful thank you and sincere goodbyes to the hospital staff at Colchester. Bob travelled via ambulance to his new destination. I followed him in my car and met him at Northwick on the Flemming Ward. We arrived about 1pm and Bob had already texted Jim to say that he had arrived. Bob was all settled on the unit in Ward B Bay one. Team Bob was updated and, like before, all visits were coordinated.

Tuesday [25/02/2020]

Sue: *Bob's all settled in! When people visit could they please check if Bob has any washing and either wash for him or drop it off to me to wash/return clean on your next visit. This will help ensure he has enough clean clothes. Whoever is going next could you please collect some more of his clothes from me, as he only has enough tops up until Thursday. Thank you.*

Lauren: *Me and Jim are planning to go Saturday's as normal we can take some. xx*

Emma: *I'll go up every other Sunday! Will be going this Sunday x.*

Mike: *Emma / Julie can I alternate this with you please.*

Bob would now be busy with his program and the distance of the journey to Northwick meant it was not as easy to visit every day. I still had things I needed to do at home and be there for the dogs. Even though I wanted to visit Bob every day, it simply was not possible. I had to compromise and decided to plan my visits midweek to leave weekends free for others. So, I decided to visit Bob on Wednesdays and stay at a nearby Premier Inn so I could also visit Thursdays. Emma agreed to stay the night at mine to look after the dogs for those days.

The unit consisted of many teams from physio, occupational and speech therapists, nursing teams, doctors, consultants, benefit and finance advisers, cleaners, catering and many more. All of them worked so well together to make everything run smoothly. It was heart-warming to see Bob work so hard with these teams. He had a full and strict timetable of activities to follow, many of which I captured on video, just like I had done in the early days on the Stroke Unit at Colchester. By doing this, Bob was able to see how much he was improving, and he was also enjoying visits from his family and friends.

Bob's parents recall their first visit to see Bob at Northwick. They travelled by train and caught the 9.20am from Colchester arriving at Liverpool Street Station, then took the Metropolitan Line to Northwick Park. It took about ten minutes to walk to the hospital from there which was well signposted. Once they were on the unit, a lady approached them, "Can I help you?" she asked.

John replied, "We're looking for our son Robert on Ward B."

She replied, "Oh, you mean Bob, I'm his doctor let me take you to him, he's doing so well." John and Daphne followed as the doctor led the way. Bob's parents were so pleased to see how well Bob had settled in.

As visits continued, time was moving at a vast speed. It was now

March and Bob continued to work really hard on his plan, smashing the boundaries yet again! Everyone was helping to keep things moving with a steady flow of fresh washed and ironed clothes and replenished toiletries along with lots of love and support. Some days, Bob and I would go into the communal room to eat lunch. They had tea and coffee making facilities, a TV, books, and lots of games. Bob liked that room as he could see Wembley Stadium from the window. I remember Jim told his dad the League Cup final match between Manchester City and Aston Villa was scheduled on 1ˢᵗ March and kick off was 4.30pm. Bob can recall hearing the crowds cheer as he sat there eating his tea that day.

Tuesday [03/03/2020]

Julie: *Visited Robert with Mitch and Mum. He's in good spirits and chatting well. His speech is improving every time I see him. He ate his dinner and then pushed himself to the gym. They said he cycled 20 minutes on the exercise bike and was really pleased with himself. He is looking forward to seeing Sue tomorrow.*

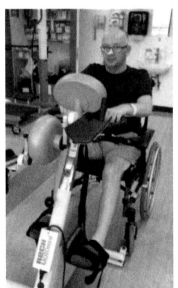

Thursday [05/03/2020]

Sue: *Bob was a bit tired yesterday but really good today. He decided not to order lunch from the hospital canteen, he wanted to buy a sandwich from M&S. I took him in wheelchair to the shops, he chose a prawn sandwich, cheese puffs & Maltesers. We also visited Hospital Friends shop and Bob bought his Mum a Mother's Day card and gift (a lovely silk scarf), it was nice he was able to choose this himself. He* *ordered salmon from the hospital canteen for dinner tonight. We attended the gym this afternoon with the occupational health team, I've posted a couple more videos of Bob on exercise bike. A meeting to update is also scheduled for 2nd April for me and Bob to attend with a target discharge date of May 11th.*

Jim: *He's like Bradley Wiggins! That's good in time for wedding!*

As Bob was doing so well, we both decided it was time to add him to his own 'Team Bob' WhatsApp group.

Monday [09/03/2020]

Bob: *Hi everyone, I'm still going* 😄😄👍

Sal: *Bob! Think you'll be able to race Andy on his bike soon what a phenomenal man you are!*

Liz: *Hello Bob! Really pleased that you are progressing so well. We are all so happy with how far you have come in such a short time xx*

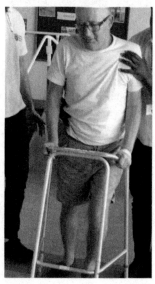

Sue: *Not only will you be walking Emma up the aisle I can also see a dad dance happening!*

Powelly: *Great to see you doing so well Roberto. Hope you're doing ok and keep that determination going, can't wait to witness you walk Emma down that aisle.*

Jackie: *Amazing achievements from an amazing person xxx*

Flis & Smithy: It's so uplifting seeing this Sue, well done, they are working him quite hard but it's paying off.

Bob had also moved through the various levels of the solid food trials and was now able to have normal consistency and unlimited water. He was only having food through his tube at night and, once he had tolerated normal meals for a few days, they said the feeding tube would be removed.

I visited as often as I could and every Wednesday after spending the day with Bob, I checked in to the hotel just down the road from the hospital. It meant I could then join him on Thursday for his early morning and daily timetable activities. I stayed all day both days and, by doing this, I saw and learnt a lot about the various exercises Bob had to do. I was also able to encourage him and spur him on to achieve his goals.

On one particular day, a lovely man introduced himself and explained his role was to help explore any financial worries we may have encountered, especially as Bob was unable to continue working and our income would now be affected. Bob and I had always been in employment and financially stable, however, our circumstances had now changed, and how we would manage financially in the future was on my mind. I have to say he was very kind and respectful as he explained that Bob was in a position to qualify for certain disability benefits. He said he could help us to complete any forms and provide medical notes as well. He was very understanding about the situation we now found ourselves in and it was clear he wanted to help us. It didn't take long and gave us some comfort that the support was out there.

He also helped Bob to apply for the disability blue badge as this would be essential to support his needs. I was aware of the blue badge and benefit system as I had supported clients of my own when applying in the past. Although I could have completed the forms, the benefit system had changed in recent years, plus my head was not in the right place to research anything new, so I was grateful of the support he gave as it made things so much easier giving me the time to support Bob with his rehabilitation program.

Bob continued to work hard in the gym, but as the level of intensity on exercises increased further, Bob's brain was adjusting and again he was feeling the unpleasant effects of dizziness and vomiting, so much so that his feeding tube became dislodged and fell out. Bob was given more anti-sickness medication to counteract those unpleasant effects and, as he was able to eat normally, they decided that the feeding tube was no longer needed and didn't need to be put back in, so on 11th March it was gone for good! Everything

was going great and I could see how much and how quickly Bob was recovering, as did our family and friends. On our visits, we often took Bob to the café in his free time, I think this was important and a lovely treat which he seemed to enjoy a lot, especially a cup of tea and his favourite prawn sandwiches!

On the days I couldn't visit Bob, I would keep in touch via phone and text and often sent him photos of Honey and Archie, just to keep him connected to them as they were not able to visit him in this hospital.

I couldn't believe it had been nearly four weeks already since Bob had been admitted to the rehab unit. I was also astonished by how much he had achieved so far and how quickly. However, worrying news of a global pandemic was emerging and reports of a new deadly disease were spreading across the globe. Covid 19 was starting to hit the UK with disastrous effects!

Chapter Ten:

Covid Pandemic and a Race Against Time

As the pandemic cases had started to increase in the UK, the news channels were reporting on the outbreaks in different regions. The public had been advised to stay at home if they had any symptoms to avoid the spread. While the media continued to report news of the many deaths occurring around the world, Italy, France, and Spain had already gone into lockdown. As the virus continued to sweep across the UK, it was inevitable that we'd be next!

I could already see a change in the surroundings and the impact at Northwick Hospital. On my visits to see Bob, the hospital corridors were becoming occupied with people whose expressions and smiles were hidden, as they wore face masks in the hope of protection. I also wore face masks and would wash my hands and sanitised with every door and contact made to surfaces. I avoided the lifts and took the stairs up six floors instead, as I wanted to be able to keep moving and avoid confined spaces in case someone coughed or sneezed. I noticed the hospital staff were washing their hands continuously. I also made sure Bob had hand gel and told him to use it and to sanitise before and after meals as well. I did not wish to worry him, but I had to make him aware of the pandemic in order to help him stay safe.

Although many of our friends and family wanted to continue to support Bob, we decided that visiting should stop. In fact, Pete and Lisa were one of the last of our friends to visit Bob. They were on their usual weekend visit to see Bob at Northwick, when we learnt of the news that the first case of Covid 19 was confirmed in Colchester. The weekend of 14th and 15th March was the last weekend that Bob received visits from family and friends, as hospitals only allowed one visitor to a bed in the days that followed. For as long as I was allowed to, I continued to visit him.

On Monday 16th March, the Prime Minister advised against "non-essential" travel, urging people to avoid pubs and clubs and to work from home if they can.

Below are a few messages from Team Bob WhatsApp group which gives an indication of what was emerging.

Sunday [15/03/2020]

Cheryl: *We only know numbers now from who is in hospital. They don't know how many are isolating as you don't contact 111 unless you're still ill over the 7 days. I'm a school nurse and the numbers of kids now off sick has doubled in just a day!*

Monday [16/03/2020]

Sue: *A suspected case of Coronavirus has been identified on level 6 in the Rehab Ward in Bay C. Bob is now in Bay F. All groups have been cancelled to avoid the spread, but one-to-one physio and speech and language is to continue for now. They have not stopped visiting as of yet, so I still plan to go Wednesday. But Bob will keep us updated on visiting protocol.*

Jim: *Most hospitals are only allowing one visitor per bed now too.*

Sal: *On my ward we can only have one visitor per bed. This came into effect yesterday.*

Unfortunately, Covid 19 was starting to spread at Northwick and had in fact made the local news. Due to the outbreak, a decision to get Bob home was made. This meant Bob's rehabilitation would subsequently be cut short, however the threat of contracting Covid 19 made coming home a priority. Bob had received just four weeks of in-patient neurorehabilitation. Miraculously, he had made remarkable improvements with his transfers, including from bed to wheelchair to walking frame and back again. This made the decision to allow Bob to be discharged early more realistic.

On Tuesday 17th March, I received a phone call from the Occupational Health Therapist who said that, because of the risk of Coronavirus, they were looking to do a home visit with Bob on the Monday to access him in his home. He would then have to go back to hospital but they would arrange a discharge date as soon as possible.

After the assessment, they would make a referral to Essex Cares for the provision of equipment to be delivered to our bungalow as we would need specialist equipment to support his recovery and living at home. As the unit was not able to achieve the physiotherapy goals outlined in his care plan, a recommendation for a referral to the communal physio team, occupational health team and speech therapy were also discussed.

Tuesday [17/03/2020]

Bob: *They just checked my height and weight for my Colchester wheelchair.*

Sue: *I'm going up tomorrow in the day to see Bob and take fresh new clothes and will come home the same day, as I don't think it's wise to stay in the hotel because of the risk of catching Covid. I will keep you posted on any discharge date which has been*

*decided to be bought forward as they believe Bob will be at less
risk of contracting Covid if home.*

Mike: *How will he get the support? Will it be via home visits from
OTs?*

Sue: *Yes, they will arrange community visits with the local team
here. Pray that lockdown doesn't happen before then* 🙏

Emma: *As long as he gets enough support from community when
he's home!*

Sue: *He will, if not I'll do it, part of the home visit will be to teach
me techniques to support him. If we do go in lockdown, you and
Will can still move in as we have already discussed. It will also
help as they will know we have more than just me at home then.*

At the time, Emma and Will lived in a flat but it had no garden and
we had already discussed the possibility of them moving in with me
if lockdown were to happen. They had a cat as well and this would be
new for Archie and Honey, but we were sure they would all get used
to one another eventually.

On Wednesday 18th March I visited Bob at the hospital and had
a meeting with Jenna the OT. The home visit to check its suitability
was scheduled for the following Wednesday 25th March. This would
enable Bob's discharge as they were working towards Bob coming
home on that same Wednesday and staying home if all equipment
were in place. With this in mind, Bob's dad organised for some
wooden ramps to be made so the wheelchair would easily glide over
the door's thresholds. Bob's other friend Clive, a lorry driver, kindly
delivered them to our home.

Rumours of the next step for closures and social restrictions for the
UK had started to spread and there were concerns the Prime Minister
was about to announce lockdown. I became concerned at the possibility

of Bob not being able to return home and worried about how this would affect his recovery and also the threat of catching the virus.

Wednesday [18/03/2020]

Flis and Smithy: *Lockdown is due to be announced at 5.00pm today. Think from what I'm being told it starts Friday.*

Cheryl: *I think that will be at the weekend and schools to close on Friday first then that will follow.*

Mike: *I think it's more likely that London will be on lockdown before any other place in the UK. This has happened in other countries like Italy and Spain where the hotspots are locked down before anywhere else.*

On Thursday 19th March, I visited Bob again. Lockdown was fast approaching. This meant the time scale for the delivery of Essex Cares equipment to be implemented in time was starting to look unrealistic. We were also told that, due to Bob's level of care needs, we would ideally need more than one person to safely facilitate his needs at home. As it was just me living at home with Bob, we needed a Plan B and fast.

With the death toll rising and hospital wards filling up with Covid patients, everyone sensed that lockdown was coming sooner than the government were anticipating or would admit to and I wasn't prepared to lose the opportunity to get Bob home before lockdown was imposed. I asked Jenna to advise me on what equipment I would need in the bungalow to allow Bob to come home. Jenna gave me a list and I took photos of the hospital equipment on the ward. I told her I would sort it out and I would email her and also text Bob with news to let her know. Then I immediately left the hospital. It was a race against time to get Bob home, but I had a plan. Near to where I lived was a local mobility shop and I was heading straight for it.

As I arrived, I parked the car and went into the mobility shop armed with my credit card. I explained the situation to the staff and gave them the list and photos of the items required. In order to enable Bob to come home, I bought a swivel bather, an over toilet frame/commode, a raised toilet seat, roller walking frame, a wheelchair and grab rails plus various other small items to support Bob's care needs. Half an hour later I had purchased all the equipment, loaded the car, and then returned home.

I started to place all the equipment where it was needed. In the main bathroom I placed the raised seat on the toilet and the swivel bath seat over the bath. I then put the shower stall and toilet frame in the bedroom en suite. I had also contacted Bob's work mate, Chris, to arrange for him to fit the grab rails in the bathrooms for me. Without hesitation, Chris arrived shortly afterwards so that everything was done prior to the OT's assessment.

I then took photos of everything and sent these via email to Jenna. I also texted these to Bob as well. I told him to let Jenna know just in case she hadn't picked up the email. Bob was on the case and it wasn't long before Jenna emailed me back. She was happy with the equipment and said she would try to arrange for Bob's discharged the following day and would organise hospital transport so she and a colleague could bring Bob home. Jenna explained they were waiting for his medication to be organised. It was the final piece of the puzzle needed to allow his discharge in time for the next day. Once at the bungalow, they would need to check the equipment. In the assumption it would all be ok, which she seemed to think it would be from the photos supplied, then Bob could be discharged and stay home.

As they had taught Bob how to transfer with two people and we didn't have the quick move return equipment yet, the condition of discharge was that there would be two people in the home until the quick move equipment arrived. I explained Emma and Will were moving in the next day and would stay for a few weeks.

I knew friends and family were waiting for news and hoping Bob could come home and as usual. I updated Team Bob.

Thursday [19/03/2020]

Sue: *All equipment in. Jenna has worked so hard to get everything sorted her end and I've received an email from her, she said it's all systems go, and she is going to go in early tomorrow before her shift to check on meds and chase up if needed. What a lovely lady!*

Jim: *Great news! Well done Mum and well done Dad xx*

John & Doreen: *Great news Sue, love John & Doreen x*

Lauren: *Yay such good news xx*

Gwen: *Well done to both of you; this is brilliant news xx*

Sal & Andy: *So blooming pleased for you both!*

Jackie: *You two are an inspiration to us all xx*

Powelly: *Well done Sue, great work from start to finish to finally get the legend home. Well done also to the main man, who has worked so hard to get himself to the standard to go home. Superb achievement all round. xx*

Heidi: *Absolutely inspirational xxx*

Cheryl: *Great job Sis, good news he will have homemade jelly yes, I have some orange.*

Max: *Great news on Bob coming home.*

Sue: *Have to laugh! Here's Bob's order for tea tomorrow! Salmon and soya sauce plus rice if we have any please x.*

Julie: At least it's not pasta! Have u told him there is a ration on toilet rolls?

Sue: Yes, he said no problem, the kids asked what they could get me for Mother's Day! So, think we got that sorted lol.

It had been a long day, but we'd done it! Everything was in place. Bob's dad had kindly cut the lawn and the garden was looking lovely, the trees and plants were starting to awaken as the hint of spring was on its way once more. I was excited at the thought that Bob would be home the next day, but also a little apprehensive. Surprisingly, I slept quite well that night.

Chapter Eleven:

Coming Home

Early the next morning on Friday 20th March, I received a call from Jenna to say that Bob's meds were ready, the hospital transport was all set. They would be leaving at 9.30am, hoping for an ETA of about 11.30am. I decided to walk the dogs before Bob, Jenna and her colleague arrived as I knew Archie and Honey would be so excited to see their dad and I wanted to make sure they had released some of their excess energy.

Friday [20/03/2020, 08:20:41]

Bob: *Homeward bound happy days (after breakfast that is)!!*

Simon: *Safe journey and welcome home Bob*

Heidi & Rich: *Just the best news to wake up to! Go Bob and Sue!* ♥ *Enjoy breakfast xxx*

Pete & Lisa: *Great so exciting for you all xx*

After I returned from the dog walk, I remembered I had some

bunting in the shed and, knowing I had a little time to spare, I decided to decorate the front of the bungalow. I also made a sign saying, 'Welcome Home Bob!' As I stood on the mini step ladder attaching the poster to the window, I heard a car pull up on the driveway, I turned around to see Jenna in the front passenger seat next to the driver and Bob was in the back with Jenna's colleague. We smiled and said hello and then I got the wheelchair and they helped Bob into our home.

The dogs were so excited to see their dad and he was so pleased to see them as well. Once the dogs had said their hellos to everyone, Jenna and her colleague helped Bob to transfer from the wheelchair to the sofa and then taught me the same technique. It didn't take long before Bob and I had cracked it. They then checked the equipment in the bungalow and were happy everything was in place.

[20/03/2020, 11:16:49]

Bob: *I'm home* 🏡 👍

Totty: *Woohoo congratulations and stay safe xx*

Sal & Andy: *Bet it feels grand Bob!*

Gwen: *Yay good to see you Bob xx*

Jim: *Great to see you home Dad.*

Mike & Charlie: *Welcome home Dad - Woohoo Bob!*

Lauren: *Welcome home!!!*

Julie: *Fantastic, you cared for my brother so well Sue, thank you from the bottom of my heart.*

Powelly: *Welcome home mate.* 😎

Maxine: *Love it nice to see you home Bob, bet the dogs were pleased to see you* 🖤🖤

Flis & Smithy: *Fabulous WELCOME HOME!! so lovely seeing these photos of you xx*

Jackie: *Welcome home Bob, it's lovely that your home together again xxx*

Bob: *Thanks everyone* 👍😀

By this time Emma had arrived and, although Will was still at work, they knew Emma and Will were moving in and were happy to discharge Bob back into my care. As they left, we thanked them for all they had done to get Bob home safe and away from the risk of Covid. I will be forever grateful to those two ladies for making that possible. Later that evening, as we watched the news on TV, they reported that Northwick Park Hospital had declared a "critical incident" due to an insurge of patients being admitted with coronavirus. Just three days later on 23rd March, the Prime Minster announced England's first national lockdown.

[20/03/2020]

Sue: *Well, a good first day! Bob's had tea we managed to transfer from wheelchair to dining table. And a few times during the day from settee to wheelchair to bathroom and back again. An evening watching tele and Bob is now settled and enjoying the comfort of his own bed. We had a few laughs along the way at comical moments working it all out together and I have to say, it's great to be able to laugh together about it with such a positive attitude. Good night all and sweet dreams. XX*

The first night we muddled through as I helped Bob to bathe and get into bed. The following morning Bob was reluctant to get up and I let this go at first, as I thought he must be tired after all he'd just been through. However, I knew the importance of keeping the physio and exercises going, especially as his brain still needed to learn and continue to reconnect pathways. It was the only way Bob had a chance to improve his mobility and quality of life.

The second morning Bob was much the same and again said he did not want to get up. I had not fought for all this time to get Bob home and then stop there. He had done so well, and I knew he had more to do. I was not prepared for this to be his limit or indeed mine. I started to feel overwhelmed at that prospect and became upset. With my emotions running high, tears began falling down my face and as I left the room, I yelled, "This is just as f***ing hard for me as it is for you, you know!" I'd never spoken to Bob like that before.

I stood in the hallway for a second trying to hold back the tears. Emma was preparing breakfast in the kitchen and I did not want her to see me upset, but I just couldn't contain it. As I entered the kitchen, Emma asked what was wrong. I told her I felt so awful for swearing and telling her dad off but explained that if he didn't get up, he'd never get better and we'd just be stuck like this. She immediately gave me a big hug and said, "We'll work it out, Mum."

I made a cup of tea and then took it into Bob and we both hugged. I'd never sworn at him like that before and even though I felt bad about it, it was the best thing I could have ever done. Throughout this journey so far, I'd always tried not to get upset in front of Bob as he needed to know I was strong and coping, but in this instance it was important to share that all this actually affected me too. It was the push he needed to give him a purpose to get up each morning. If he couldn't do it for himself, he would now do it for me.

Over the next six weeks, Emma and Will took care of everything to do with the house, garden and chores, the dog walks and cooking etc. This left me completely free to care for Bob and concentrate on his care and physio exercises. I had no experience of this before and there was no set plan. I just worked with Bob and repeated the exercises I had seen him do at the hospitals and we took it from there. But somehow, I had a sense God was guiding me!

No one knew how long lockdown would last, but Bob and I continued every day working on the various physio exercises and when Bob didn't initially achieve the objective, I encouraged him again to continue and with great patience he would improve and overcome. Bob would listen and try again; it was so humbling to watch.

I adapted the home to cater for Bob as much as I could in order for him to feel as empowered as possible. Bob would wheel himself in his chair around the bungalow. I moved his cereals and biscuits into the cupboards he could reach and assorted items such as milk and ice-cream on the lowest shelves in the fridge and freezer compartments, so he was able to help himself to his favourite things.

As part of his rehabilitation, Emma would work with Bob on his speech therapy and she also got Bob involved in baking cakes, encouraging him to use his left hand to stir the mixture to help strengthen the control that had been lost. We gave him jigsaw puzzles, Lego, and sudoku puzzles to do and played dominos and Jenga. He would also work on his leg muscles in a seating position on the sofa using a little exercise floor cycle. On nice days we would go into the garden. Bob would sit in the wheelchair and throw footballs for the dogs and we would play catch. All of these things helped hand and eye coordination improving his fine motor movement skills even further. Rainbows also made an appearance during these amazing times of rehabilitation, always a comforting sign for me.

Although things were improving for us at home, unfortunately the pandemic was crippling the country. Sadly, many lives had been lost and many restrictions had been put in place, including a restriction on the number of mourners that could attend funerals, which was heart-breaking for loved ones.

Hospitality was also affected with many social events banned. The 2020 spring and summer wedding season was hit hard. Like many other couples who had cancelled their respective weddings, Emma and Will also had no choice but to postpone their wedding too.

I know how upset we all were, especially Emma and Will, but there was nothing we could do, except contact all the suppliers to try to secure and coordinate a new date. I told Emma we should do this sooner rather than later as everyone else would be in the same boat. After a few phone calls, Emma and I managed to secure a new date and the wedding was now scheduled to take place on 1st August 2021. Luckily the main suppliers and venue were able to align.

Their original wedding date had only been a couple of months away. I had always been determined Bob would walk Emma down the aisle. I comforted myself with the thought that at least postponing the wedding would give Bob more time and who knew? We might even now get a dad-daughter dance too!

Like the rest of the country, people were keeping connected with family and friends remotely and zoom meetings became the new way to stay in touch. Each week, our families would connect via zoom for some really fun quiz evenings. I always looked forward to these, especially as Cheryl provided us with great entertainment trying to get to grips with this modern technology. Out of the blue Cheryl would have virtual props that would appear on her screen like sunglasses or bunny ears. This really made us all laugh, especially because she had no idea why or how they were appearing; I still have those videos saved and they still make me laugh to this day!

I remember how lovely it was to receive kind video messages from Heidi, Rich, Harry and Gwennie, all wishing Bob well and supporting us both. We had met this lovely family just the once, while on holiday in Norfolk back in the summer of 2019, and we had felt a special connection straight away, remaining friends ever since. Even though we hadn't had the opportunity to meet up again since Bob's stroke and the Covid outbreak, we kept connected via text and video messages and also in the Team Bob WhatsApp chat, where they could see how well Bob was doing.

By April, Bob was managing to walk around the bungalow a little way with the aid of his frame. We hardly had to support his balance any more as his brain was starting to adjust and learning to control it. Bob was doing so well, but I felt we had reached a plateau, and I wasn't sure what to try next. I started to research new physio and balancing exercises on the internet and found some really good ones which helped to raise the game even more. One in particular was placing yellow post-it notes on a wall in the form of the number 5, as on a dice. Bob then had to stand in front and stare at the centre one and try to touch the other post-it notes, first with his right hand and then his left, while always keeping his eye on the note in the centre. This amazingly helped him to relearn the skill of balancing while standing still.

One of us always stood near ready to catch him, as sometimes he would wobble a bit when he became tired. It was absolutely amazing to see how well the brain could adapt and relearn!

17/04/2020]

> **Sue:** *So today is 4 weeks since Bob came home from hospital! I know both myself and Bob were determined to work hard with rehabilitation and Emma and Will have been a huge help with this process in supporting us too! Bob is unable at present to receive community physio and OT home visits, so we have tried to implement this as best we can ourselves. I always had faith that Bob would walk again and still believe this but always knew it would take a lot of hard work and time. I can't, however, believe just how far Bob has come in the last 4 weeks, especially as we have no experience of this type of rehabilitation. But today we thought we would try and push the boundaries further to help Bob with the next step to walking independently with walking frame.*

Even though I had looked at exercises on the internet, I felt I needed more ideas and possibly different equipment now. We hadn't heard from the Community Physio Team and I thought this was because of lockdown but decided to email them anyway. We learnt later that Bob's referral had been lost in all the chaos of the pandemic. In the meantime, I asked family and friends if anyone had a treadmill we could borrow. My cousin kindly gave us his one and, along with my uncle, they brought it over to the bungalow. This really helped Bob make great progress.

Spring was well under way and days outside in the garden were welcomed. It was nice to sit outside in the fresh air with a cup of tea and the kiss of the warm sun upon our faces. The weather was kind to us, and we enjoyed delicious barbecues on glorious days. Will became the BBQ king as he cooked steaks to perfection and Emma made the most delightful lemon meringue pies and desserts.

As fast as April had come and gone, the month of May was truly upon us, and with it many family celebrations. A steady flow of birthday and Mother's Day cards, cakes and gifts were arriving at the door and Bob received his disability blue badge too.

The community physio teams had made contact and home visits were due to begin. We also received some really lovely and exciting news as Jim and Lauren facetimed us to say they were expecting a baby in December. When I learnt the due date happened to be my late Mum's birthday, I knew it was a sign from the heavens! Our first grandchild was on the way, which meant Bob was going to be a grandad and I was going to be a nana!

I said to Bob he would need to work harder on his physio if he had any chance of keeping up with the new arrival once the baby started to crawl. We both laughed. I did think this was also another great incentive to encourage Bob to keep moving forward.

[06/05/2020]

Bob: *I've had first visit (assessment) from local physio and OT team, they are back to start exercises next week but could see Matron Sue had done the hard work as already walking with frame.*

And so that's how I earned the affectionate name of Matron, which has stuck to this day. Thanks, Bob! Now that the community team were coming on board, we all agreed that it was time for Emma and Will to move back into their own home. I cannot thank them enough for all they did for us both and especially in lockdown.

[09/05/2020]

Sue: *Emma and Will are moving out today. They have been fantastic in supporting us. I know for sure that if they had not moved in, Bob's progress wouldn't have been as much as it is now.*

I was able to concentrate on supporting Bob with physio and OT in the first few vital weeks at home, while Emma and Will supported with cooking and dog walks and general household duties. As Bob improved and became more independent, Emma was able to do some physio as well, while I took a break with a dog walk. Bob and I feel confident we are able to manage as a couple, plus the community team are now on board. We would like to say thank you to Emma and Will, from the bottom of our hearts. Jim, Lauren, Mike, and Charlie, you have also been a great support, but because of Covid I know this has restricted you to a certain degree. You are all wonderful children to us, and we love you and your partners all so very much.

On Sunday 24th May 2020, the day that should have been Emma and Will's wedding day, the country was still in lockdown, but as a family we all decided to have a party via Zoom to acknowledge the day. We had all prepared ourselves mini buffets and dressed up for the occasion. Bob and I had also been working on Bob's goal to walk Emma down the aisle. I am proud to say that, had the wedding gone ahead on this day, Bob would have achieved this!

With Bob in his suit and me in a dress, we posted a video on Team Bob of Bob walking arm in arm with me across the lounge as we practiced the wedding march. I always maintained he would do this, and he did! Although the actual wedding could not go ahead, Bob had achieved his goal and we knew that, come 1ˢᵗ August 2021,

Bob would be walking his daughter down that aisle and it was now time to work on his dance moves!

Over the next few weeks, the community teams started working on the next level with Bob. Speech therapy began and was done remotely via Zoom. Physios, Tom and Megan became regular visitors to our home and relentlessly worked with Bob to achieve even more milestones and goals. As you can see from the photos, PPI was always worn by the team and strict sanitising measures and mask wearing continued. Even Archie got in on the act!

Bob was doing so well with physio and OT exercises that he was able to achieve much more. I will never forget the day he got out of bed one morning and went into the kitchen with his walking frame. When he came back very slowly with his frame, he was balancing a cup of tea for me on it! Prior to his stroke, this was something Bob had always done every morning without fail. Although half of the tea ended up on the walking frame tray, the tea that remained in the cup tasted great. It was the best cup of tea ever! I was so touched by this; it made my eyes leak. I found the little things like that meant so much and Bob must have felt really good that he was able to do this for me as well.

As time moved on, it began to look like England had started to get a grip on the Covid pandemic. In May, the laws were slowly relaxed. From the 13th May, people were allowed to leave home for outdoor recreation and on 1st June, people were permitted to meet outside in groups of up to six people. It wasn't long before Bob was able to visit the gym at the hospital where they had much more equipment and

Megan and Tom continued their excellent work with Bob.

For a while it looked like we were coming out of the pandemic, however, with the winter months approaching, cases started to increase again and another lockdown began. The NHS was under so much pressure. To show our appreciation and public support for all the doctors and nurses, the nation would clap on their doorsteps every Thursday evening. Bob and I would go outside alongside with our neighbours who had gathered to applaud and show appreciation to all those putting their lives on the line for everyone.

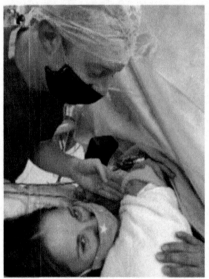

In November 2020, our lives changed forever, and in a good way! On Friday 6th, our beautiful baby granddaughter Imogen was born. Although born prematurely, she proved to be a fighter just like her grandad Bob. The second lockdown meant more restrictions and giving birth in the middle of a pandemic was now very different to the norm. However, Lauren and Jim were brilliant and took to parenthood so well, despite the unusual circumstances they found themselves in. Immy had to stay in the Special Care Baby Unit for a while until she was well enough to come home. Lauren was not allowed to stay at the hospital with her for the duration. Both Lauren and Jim visited their daughter daily, but they had to visit her separately as only one parent was allowed on the unit at a time. On 19th November, Jim and Lauren brought their baby girl home. To keep everyone safe and from risk of

catching the virus, we followed the rules set by the government and did not go inside their house. The first time we physically saw our baby granddaughter was through their family home lounge window. Soon afterwards, we met them outside for walks, as this was allowed at the time. Lauren always made sure the plastic rain hood cover was on the pram. This was a good idea and gave Immy extra protection. We never ever touched or held Immy at this stage, because we wanted her to stay safe.

Under normal circumstances we would have been able to visit them and hold our new baby granddaughter. The pandemic changed all of that. Although we could not physically be with our new grandchild, Jim always made sure we were able to see Imogen via video and facetime which meant a great deal to us.

On Christmas Day 2020, families were able to form a temporary bubble and meet for that one day. Bob and I both did Covid tests to make sure we were safe to visit and, as a precaution, as well as washing our hands often, we wore masks too. I will always treasure and hold this day in  my heart forever, because this was the first time we were able to hold our precious baby granddaughter.

Pictured in Bob's arms on Christmas Day is Imogen, the grandchild that Jim had told his dad to live and fight for back in November 2019 while trying to get him to respond from the coma.

As hard as it was for us all, as a family, we did stick to the rules and restrictions that were set out by the government, even though some of those government senior members at the time clearly didn't.

Again, time was moving fast. 2020 had been an eventful year to say the least and New Year's Eve was soon upon us. However, this one was different to the last, as this time Bob was by my side and we were able to see it in together. With the arrival of the new year, Bob continued to work hard to keep on improving and I have to say how proud I am of Bob for his perseverance, strength, and sheer determination to keep going. It started to look like there was light at the end of the tunnel. The pandemic was changing, and things looked brighter as news of a vaccine hit the headlines. However, a new variant of Covid 19 known as Omicron was sweeping the country, which led to a third national lockdown in England on January 4th, 2021.

Although we did not know it then, 2021 was the year we would win the fight against Covid. In the months to follow, a national vaccination program was rolled out. Covid 19 cases began to drop and restrictions were gradually lifted. There were still restrictions on weddings. With Emma and Will's due to take place in August, we were watching this closely. May 2021 weddings had a restriction of thirty guests, but things turned around quite quickly. On 19th July 2021, lockdown ended and for the Bloomfield family good times followed!

Chapter Twelve:

Celebrations and Time to Party

Sunday 1st August 2021 was a momentous day indeed! And one full of immense joy and celebration as Emma and Will were married.

Yes, not only was Bob able to walk Emma down the aisle, but he was also able to deliver his father of the bride speech and dance with his beautiful daughter!

As well as the wedding, in the months and years to follow we got to celebrate many happy occasions and Bob continued to achieve much more!

As long as Bob was happy to accept he would need to make some adjustments and introduce certain aids and equipment to help support this, then there was nothing to stop him from being able to continue with the hobbies and recreational activities that he had once enjoyed.

Bob invested in a mobility scooter which was really good for him. He has learnt to walk again but is limited to a certain distance, so the scooter is great when he accompanies me on a long walk with the dogs and also to the local shops.

Bob also uses the scooter on the golf course sometimes instead of a golf buggy. It has enabled him to continue to socialise with his golf friends and also move around the course.

Bob has learnt to walk again, swim again, and returned to golf in the summer months, plus he has taken up a new hobby of indoor bowls to keep him occupied in the winter.

After passing his driving assessment, Bob regained his license and was able to start driving again. His car was an automatic anyway, which is extremely useful to him now and he also adapted his car by fitting an electric hoist to help lift his mobility scooter in and out of the car with ease. A steering wheel spinner has also been fitted.

He continues to enjoy special times with family and friends, including BBQs at home and meals out, as well as venturing on holiday to the Norfolk Broads and getting to enjoy more holidays with both family and friends.

One of the holidays which was incredibly special to us, was presented by Jim on Christmas Day back in 2020, gifted to us by members of 'Team Bob'. They had organised and booked a weekend away, scheduled for September 2021 for Bob and me to stay in a beautiful little cottage in Norfolk. We were also given vouchers to enjoy an evening meal at a lovely local restaurant, as well as a boat trip on the Norfolk Broads and tickets to visit Thrigby Hall Wildlife Gardens.

It was so heart-warming to receive such a truly kind and thoughtful gift and was in fact our first time away on holiday together since Bob's stroke. It was such a lovely thing for 'Team Bob' to do and we had the best time! I honestly believe that, if it wasn't for the support Bob and I received from all of our family, friends, the remarkable medical and physio teams, and staff who looked after Bob at all three hospitals, together with their respective community teams, then none of this would have been possible.

With this in mind, Bob and I wanted to do something special to say "Thank You" to everyone who helped us in some way. So, on 26th November 2022, we decided to invite everyone to a celebration with fine dining and dancing, which was held at Colchester Golf Club. The evening was just magical, and everyone relished the celebrations. I was touched to see that Will wore the blue Hugo Boss top Bob had bought him for the Secret Santa back in 2019. I was also touched by the love and support conveyed to the Bloomfield family and the speeches from Bob, his dad and best mate Pete, copies of which are in the back of this book.

Although 'Team Bob' had many members, not everyone had met each other in person and it was nice to get everyone all together. As well as catching up with each other, our friends and family were also able to speak with the medical teams and convey their thanks and appreciation for looking after their dear friend Bob. It was evident how grateful everyone was to them when loud applause echoed around the room during the speeches.

I also had the opportunity to speak with Aktham (Dr El-rekaby) that night and learnt that his decision to authorise another scan so urgently was not only based on his duty of care to Bob's sudden deterioration but also other factors played their part! This is what he told me!

"Let me mention two things here.

Firstly, Bob's case was unique to me, he came in just at the right moment at the peak of my career. At the time I was reading about similar cases in literature, there was a case presentation similar to Bob's. A headache is not a common presentation or indicator for deterioration, but at the time you asked me, I had a train of thought and knowledge that headaches could be a marker for early deterioration in cases like Bob's. So, if this was not picked up, we might end with a different result. In these moments, I believe and listen to the family's feelings and concerns, and to my sixth sense, what we call over obsession or cleverness. The key was listening and applied knowledge. We know that Bob's case is uncommon not an everyday presentation.

Secondly, I have personal experience of this rare type of stroke. My wife's family member collapsed while she was at work and suffered the same type of stroke at same site in brain and went through almost the same as Bob. The difference for her was that the hospital stroke service that she received care from runs in one place. Therefore, she was able to be treated and admitted to ITU where she had a craniectomy and was put in an induced coma for 10 days. This was all done at the same centre. I would love to have a similar centre here, where we could provide everything all under one roof to treat my patients in the same way.

The fact is that time matters in a stroke and particularly in the site like the brainstem (back of brain where respiratory centre site is) it's vital. This was the same in Bob's case. A delay in diagnosis or action would end in a completely different result. Now at the time the CT head scan was done, it was clear Bob started to deteriorate quickly and this was not uncommon just like this case as I have mentioned ref brainstem on how vital this site of stroke is.

So, I was in my room doing my job and had to be precise and quick. I used my knowledge and skills to communicate with the team at Romford. I was keen to get Bob to them and mentioned my personal experience of my wife's family member, in order to give Bob the best chance. In my mind I was thinking of my wife's family member and wished at that time to have a similar outcome and care for Bob.

Honestly, in that moment I was hoping for a miracle. I wanted to give this every chance and could see how much you and your family cared. That was another drive to provide extra mile for my patient. It worked: Bob went to Queen's Hospital. The next I heard was that Bob had made it. I said that was a miracle. Miracles do happen (Angels).

I was astonished at the amount of care you and your family have given to Bob and the hard work you and all the people around Bob have done. Listening to Bob I felt he deserves merit and there are many things excellent in him, he is vibrant and spreads happiness all around him. This is Bob. I said he's made it; he's worked hard, and he will live long. I have faith in my sixth sense that he is not going to have any further issues.

I know this type of stroke is futile. I do not know the exact percentage, but we know that it's one of the bad ones. I do not like to speak about what could have happened and the possibility. But Bob is a survivor, and you are a hero to get him over this.

We have done our job and Team Bob has done theirs. We loved the celebration evening and are very happy to see Bob and you together surrounded by wonderful family and friends. And I asked your little granddaughter when she grows up to be a doctor to look after us when I and we all get older."

Bob also decided that he wanted to return to Queens' Hospital Romford to meet the surgeon Mr Raghu Vindlacheruvu who had performed the lifesaving brain surgery. A meeting was  arranged, and the surgeon was very happy to see Bob. He even arranged for Bob to meet the staff in the Critical Care Unit where

Bob had spent his days in a coma. It was quite surreal to be back there but a lovely opportunity for Bob to gain an understanding of his journey. Although he doesn't remember anything about it, he was able to relate to the things

I have written in this book. Bob said he felt it was important for the surgeon to see the outcome of all his efforts and hard work to preserve life. He felt most of the time they don't get to see this, as people move on. More importantly, he wanted to say "Thank You" to Mr Vindlacheruvu and his team for saving his life.

On another occasion our dear friend Pete also revisited the hospital with us, and we went into St Luke's Chapel where we were able to view the prayer books of 2019 and 2020. As we searched through the pages inside, we found the prayers we had both written. They had for sure definitely been answered! It was quite comforting to be back there, but also emotional as I sat in the stillness reflecting on the times I had visited this special place.

More good times followed, as in 2023 we were lucky enough to enjoy a holiday abroad, something I never thought would be possible at the time of Bob's stroke. But with the help of the travel agent, who organised assistance, we jetted off to Majorca. It was brilliant, and both Bob and I had a lovely time. Bob had also arranged to hire a mobility scooter which was there at the hotel when we arrived.

This meant we were able to explore the resort a lot more, as Bob was able to join me as I walked along the prom. We both appreciated the

opportunity and freedom this brought. Rather than feeling restricted to our hotel, we could venture out further to explore the various bars and restaurants along the coastal wall. It was lovely to sample the local tapas and refreshing drinks whilst taking in the glorious sea views.

Bob will tell you the best thing about that holiday for him was when I helped him to paddle in the sea and he could feel the sand beneath his feet, as the gentle waves splashed along the shoreline. And the best thing for me?

Well, seeing two sets of footprints in the sand of course! Those who know, know!

In December 2023 we had some surprising, but very lovely news as Emma and Will announced they were expecting their first baby due in May 2024. We were both over the moon that another lovely little grandchild was on the way!

April 4th, 2024 was another wonderful day of celebration as Jim married Lauren. The day was just perfect, it was so picturesque, and Lauren looked stunning. It was so lovely to have all the family together again! We treasure these moments!

As you can see, Bob has a fantastic quality of life and lives it to the full. None of this would have been possible without all the help, love and support we received from everyone.

I started writing this book in 2022 and it may have taken a few years to complete, but as I sit here thinking about how I will end this last chapter, I am reminded just how incredible Bob's journey has been and indeed how incredible Bob and Team Bob are!

Today is 18th May 2024 and, as I sit here applying the finishing touches, I have been given the perfect ending to this book. I am delighted to bring you the wonderful news that at 11.29 am this morning, Emma and Will became the proud parents of a beautiful baby boy!

Allow me to introduce you to the newest member of Team Bob!

Baby Milo

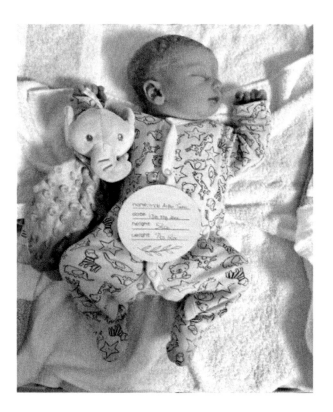

With great love, miracles are made!

Speeches

Bob's Speech - Team Bob Party

26th November 2022

Welcome:

Firstly, I'd like to welcome you all.

You've been randomly selected .... I mean specially selected for your help to my family and I in my troubles. You are all special but I'm sure you'll agree we have a guest of honor: Dr Aktham El-rekaby, my Specialty Stroke Doctor. Sue and I are delighted he could attend. He is joined by his wife and five members of his brilliant team plus two community physios who helped me.

After all the undignified things he got me to do, I'm going to ask him and his colleagues to stand up and receive a round of applause. And they say behind every successful man is a good woman, so please also be upstanding Mrs. El-rekaby and Mrs. Sue Bloomfield (aka Matron) (Applause)

Also, someone special here is Immy. When I was in coma, I'm told Jim and Lauren said to me they were going to try for a baby and my heart monitor went up. She's two now, so we should all wave at her. In fact, she was two a few weeks ago, so I think we should sing happy birthday to her ...

Apologies:

I have a few apologies. First, I personally apologize to Sue, my family, and my friends for causing so much hassle. Secondly, I apologize for falling asleep when you all made long journeys to see me and spent hours looking for parking space.

I apologize for not remembering some of your visits, some things I remembered didn't actually happen and those that did I can't remember!

Lastly, I'd like to apologize to Carman and Chris for missing their wedding.

Thanks:

We would like to thank you all for your efforts and help. I'm sure Aktham and Matron, my affectionate name for Sue, would agree that every little thing helped in my recovery.

I would like to thank Sue for caring for me and researching physio in lockdown.

I would like to thank Emma and Will for getting married and giving me a focus for recovery and moving back in with us to allow me to come home.

I also thank Mike and Charlie for telling me they didn't like the carpets I'd just organized for them, another bleep on the heart monitor, and Jim and Lauren for bringing Immy to the world.

I would like to thank Immy for helping me walk and getting me cushions when we sit on the floor to play.

I would like to thank you all for looking after Sue and our family.

I would like to thank Aktham for wisely listening to Sue when she spotted I'd deteriorated and for organising another scan straight away, which saved my life.

I would like to thank Sue for deciding to visit me that morning, rather than walking the dogs first, and spotting my deterioration.

Thanks also goes to Jim & Lauren, Mike & Charlie, and Emma & Will for all their help and support for Sue in a very tricky time.

Also, Mum and Dad, my sister Julie, and Sue's sister Cheryl and Peter Tickner.

So, this little party is for you all as our way of saying thank you. Everything you did helped so much. I would love to mention you all but obviously can't.

Lastly a big thank you to Archie and Honey, our two dogs. Sue brought them to the hospital to help aid my recovery and Archie sat on my feeding tube and pulled it out! Since I've been home, Honey has taken on the role of 'assistance dog' and watches me wherever I go.

Funny story:
Just to show how my memories are twisted. Every evening at about 7.00pm, a nurse would give me an injection in my stomach which I believe was for blood thinning.

One morning I told Sue a nurse had been round in the evening and had given me an injection in the head. I thought that nurse was Heidi, a longstanding friend we met years ago in a pub in Norfolk, and she's a schoolteacher! That explains why my recollection of events is very poor. I have more of those stories for another time, like the time I was convinced Emma was doing a night shift on the ward and Sue staying the night to make sure she was ok.

End:
We hope you enjoy the night. If I dance too much, call a doctor. As Joe Cocker sang – we get by with a little help from our friends!

At the ladies' request we now have a disco. Unfortunately, all the male Bloomfield's have a doctor's note to say they can't dance! But I'm going to ignore that and do the first dance, but I'll need medical assistance so can all the medical team please join me on the dance floor? I'm afraid that includes you, Aktham, but I'm told you're a bit of a mover, so you'll show me up!

John's Speech - Team Bob Party

26th November 2022

Well, as Robert has been saying, we call him Robert because that's what we christened him. I'd like to say on a serious note, he's asked me to thank the NHS.

I know there are lots of problems in the NHS at the moment like lack of funding and a lot of bad press, but I can assure you, once you get to the sharp end where these lovely people are, you get incredible attention and devotion. They are so devoted to their jobs, it's a joy to see.

You realise that the people above them sometimes do things that us people don't agree with. But when you're being treated in hospital, as a lot of us know, it is first-class treatment, and I would like to thank you all.

Pete's Speech - Team Bob Party

26th November 2022

"Thank You" Bob and John.

I have to say, it's great to see so many people here to celebrate the miraculous recovery of our dear Friend Bob and so, before I forget, I would just like to thank Bob & Sue on behalf of ALL of us for organising this evening of celebration, which is such a wonderful thing to do.

When I was with Bob & Sue a few months ago, I asked if I

*could say a few words – **well, those who know me, will know it
will be more than a few words!!** And, on behalf of both 'Team
Bob' and Bob & Sue, I would like to share some of my thoughts
and memories.*

*You will all have your memories, but I just wanted to share a
few of mine AND for us all to remember the amazing journey we
are celebrating tonight.*

*We could easily be here for hours talking about Bob & Sue's
journey, but what I've tried to do is reduce it into just a few
minutes; I very much hope I've captured most things, but
inevitably I am sure there will be things which you feel are
important, that I have missed and so I apologise in advance.*

*However, this is OUR evening and Team Bob was a collective
effort and so if there is anything you'd like me to add, then please
shout it out and let us include it, let's make what I'm about to say
another joint 'Team Bob' effort!*

Hospitals & Recovery:
*Bob was admitted to Colchester hospital after collapsing at
work with a stroke on Monday 11th November 2019. We were
exchanging messages with our usual banter for two days and then
the messages stopped,*

*I'll never forget, Julie rang me to say Bob had deteriorated and
was seriously ill. I struggled to comprehend what was suddenly
happening.*

*Bob was 'blue lighted' to Queen's on Friday 15th November.
Less than a week after his stroke, Mitch rang to say things were
not good and asked if we wanted to visit Bob to say our goodbyes.
I was devastated and, again, could not comprehend this news. The
following day, at 6am, Lisa and I were driving to Romford – it
was a long, reflective, and quiet drive. I'll be honest, I was totally
distraught when I saw my best mate lying on the bed connected to
so many machines & monitors and I had to take a little time out*

to process it. We stayed with Bob for quite a while, talking to him and holding his hand before leaving.

As Bob was not responding after his emergency brain surgery, Sue and the family had made the heart-breaking decision to follow Bob's known wishes and to give consent to turn off the life support, ready for organ donation.

We were told the life support machine was going to be turned off on the morning of Friday 22nd November and so Lisa & I went to see Bob again on the Thursday, but this visit felt different from the previous one; after talking with Bob for a while, we held his hand and kissed him 'goodbye' BUT, as we walked away, we both 'independently' felt this wasn't the end - I know it might be easy to say this now - but it's the truth, we both felt Bob was 'THERE'. It was a weird, but yet a calming feeling.

The following day, I was at the University of Essex just pacing around waiting for the dreaded phone call. When it came to say the machine was not switched off because Bob had responded and opened his eyes, my tears were of joy and not sorrow. I had actually written a message for Sue and the family, which I am so pleased I never had to send.

So, what had happened? Well 20 minutes before the family were due to arrive at Queen's, the consultant called them to say the team were not sure turning off the life support would go ahead and subsequently the organ donation either, as they thought, although slight, it seemed Bob was responding with his eyes. The next 20 minutes, whilst they continued their journey, felt like an eternity for Sue and the family, with so many mixed thoughts and emotions.

Sue recalls that she walked into the room where Bob was lying there with his eyes closed looking peaceful, with the life support machine helping him to breath. She remembers praying in that instant, and she then called Bob's name. His eyes opened so wide and, although the rest of his body could not move, his eyes moved to the side where she was standing. At that moment she knew Bob *was back and knew he would recover enough to walk again.*

You all know RAINBOWS are incredibly special to Sue and have always been great signs throughout her life - a sign of HOPE. On that very day, Friday 22nd November, as the family left the house to travel to Queen's, a beautiful rainbow appeared above the house.

And so, the miracle that is Bob had begun and 'Team Bob' was born.

Bob's sister Julie did a fantastic job in coordinating the visiting rota, to ensure Bob had visitors every day. Lisa and I visited him throughout his stays in Queen's, Colchester, and Northwick Park. Lisa was great always offering to massage Bob's feet & hands and we would also attempt to give him a shave and cut his finger nails etc. Bob was always up for the massages and pampering, which I know all of those who visited him offered to do - knowing Bob, I wouldn't be surprised if YOU delayed your recovery, just so you could have more massages and pampering sessions!!

There were dark times, sad times, happy times, and 'rainbow' times across our many visits, but I have two visits to Queen's that really stick out in my mind, which I wanted to share.

The first was when we visited the chapel with Sue, and I sat down and wrote a prayer for Bob to be read out during the next service.

The second was when I was playing with a stress relief ball which had been given to Bob to help strengthen his hand muscles. I instinctively did what I would normally do, and I threw it (albeit gently) to Bob who – amazingly! - went to catch it. I guess it reminded you of your days playing cricket, Bob, because you missed it!! We did this a few times. Bob kept trying to catch it, but his timing and co-ordination was out. But then, all of a sudden, he caught it and tried to throw it back to me. We continued and he caught it again - I was overwhelmed.

Whilst Bob was in Colchester, before transferring to Northwick Park, Archie and Honey paid visits to him, which was fantastic.

I'll talk about Sue and the amazing Bloomfield family shortly; but when the Covid outbreak started to take a grip, Sue did such a fantastic job to get Bob discharged from Northwick Park on the 20th of March, three days before 'lockdown'!!! With the greatest of respect, if this hadn't happened, then Bob's recovery would have been severely hindered, to say the least.

So now the 'Home Recovery' started. We have all seen the videos of the various and relentless exercises Bob did with Sue, the family, and the fantastic physio teams and the gradual progress Bob began to make.

Emma stayed with Sue & Bob for the first 6 weeks to support her Mum and Dad.

So, fast track to today and all that Bob has achieved with Sue by his side:

- *Learning to walk again and to be able to go for walks with Archie & Honey*
- *Learning to swim again*
- *Learning to drive again*
- *Enjoying special times with family and of course enjoying quality times with Imogen and being a fantastic Granddad*
- *Enjoying special times with friends*
- *Being the proud owner of his 'fast' mobility scooter*
- *Holidays with Sue and the family*
- *A return to Golf and I'm so pleased to say Bob and I are going away next year for a golfing holiday, which is something I've always wanted to do with him.*
- *AND of course, there was Emma & Will's wedding - walking Emma down the aisle, the wedding speech and dancing with both Emma and then with Sue. Not a dry eye in the room!!*

Looking back, it really has been a miracle and such an amazing, inspirational, and humbling journey for us all to witness.

That said, I guess the only thing we were ALL hoping for, as part of your recovery, Bob, was for your singing voice to improve, but, sadly, that was clearly a bridge too far!

Bob:

Bob, you are remarkable, and I sometimes think you don't truly recognise or acknowledge all you have gone through and achieved. Your attitude and approach to what happened and your patience and determination to get better is incredible. Starting off with the 'blinks' to answer 'Yes' or 'No' to our questions and then the thumbs up and all the rehabilitation exercises in the hospitals.

I remember watching, in awe, the videos Sue posted of you at home working on the various exercises. When you didn't initially achieve the objective, with Sue's encouragement, you would continue with great patience to improve and achieve. A lesser person would have become so frustrated and wanted to have given up, but not YOU! No, you listened and tried and then tried again - it was so humbling to watch. You should feel so proud of all you have achieved and continue to achieve.

The amazing, funny, caring, trusting, loyal and dependable husband, father and friend is back. Bob is back and isn't it such a fantastic thing to be able to say?!

Sue:

Well, what can I say about Sue?!

Sue, you are an incredible lady; we all knew this before Bob's stroke, but to witness all you have gone through, all you have done, and how you have conducted yourself, is again inspirational and very humbling.

From all the emotions of the first few days and through the various stages of Bob's recovery you were dealing with so much:

Dealing with all your own feelings and emotions, trying to come to terms with all what was happening.

Remaining strong as a mother to protect your children.

Remaining strong for the other members of your family and for your friends.

To have the faith and inner strength to do all of those things and then to lead Bob's recovery, communicating and working with the hospital staff, encouraging all of us of to do the things you wanted for Bob whilst he was in hospital. And then, all your Unconditional Love, Devotion, Patience, Determination and Encouragement for Bob, working with him once he was home. This was - and remains to this day - so incredible.

As I've already said, very inspirational and humbling - such an amazing thing for all of us here this evening to witness.

Again, like Bob, I don't think you truly recognise or acknowledge all what you have gone through and achieved. You and Bob are such an amazing couple, who we all love so very much. You are a 'TEAM' and together you have achieved this remarkable recovery and continue to enrich all of our lives.

Others:
Of course, Bob and Sue were not alone on this journey.

Jim, Mike, and Emma and their wonderful partners, Lauren, Charlie, and husband Will, also played such a pivotal role in Bob's recovery and supporting Sue. The Bloomfield family, as we all know, is such a very special and loving family. I know both Bob and Sue are extremely proud of you ALL and want to thank you for all your love, support, and everything you have collectively done for them and continue to do so.

At this point, I must also mention Archie and Honey, who have also played an important part with Bob's recovery.

And of course, there is Imogen, who was just a twinkle in her parents' eyes when Bob was ill, but both Jim and Lauren told Bob to pull through, as they wanted to start a family, and their child would need a Granddad. And what a 'Granddad Bob' and 'Nana' you both are! I know how much you both enjoy such special times with Imogen and have a fantastic relationship with her.

Then there is Bob's Mum and Dad. As parents, to see your son so close to leaving you and then watching him and your daughter in-law go through so much, is unimaginable.

And Bob and Sue's respective sisters and their partners and children, who were steadfast and always there for you both.

I know Bob and Sue want to thank you for ALL your love, support and everything you have collectively done for them and continue to do so.

Bob, Sue wanted me to tell you on her behalf how very proud she is of your strength, courage, and determination and how proud she is of YOU and how much she loves you.
As I say, the Bloomfield Family, is a very special family, and are such an example to us ALL.

Sue would like a shout out to her TAG family, who were great, often cooking Sue meals, walking with her and the dogs, and supporting her emotionally, with thanks also to the rest of the Tendring Agility Group family and their hounds.

I would also like to acknowledge and give huge thanks on behalf of Bob & Sue, their families, and those of us in 'Team Bob' to the remarkable Medical & Physio Teams and all the staff who looked after Bob & Sue at the three hospitals. We all owe Bob's life to you and words cannot express our sincere gratitude. Your skill and commitment to preserve life and enable miracles like this to happen leaves us all speechless and full of admiration - "thank you!

Finally, I come to those of us in 'Team Bob'. I know from the conversations I've had with Bob & Sue, they would like me to say thank you on their behalf to all of us, for the love and support we as a 'Team' have given and continue to give to them and the Bloomfield family and for being a part of this miracle. 'Team Bob' was such a brilliant idea, enabling all of Bob's loved ones to follow his updates and progress from the very beginning. For me, it was a privilege to be part of the 'Team' and to be able to witness first-hand the miracle of Bob, the extraordinary and unconditional love for him from Sue and his family, and the love and support from all his friends.

As we all know, Bob and Sue are such an amazing couple who we all love dearly and for me they are my best friends. I can't imagine life without them and so I would like you all to raise a glass to Bob and Sue and to wish them every happiness for the future.

"TO BOB & SUE!"

Before I sit down, I have a special request. I understand we have a young man called Harry with us this evening, where is Harry? Harry, I know on a video call during the early stages of Bob's recovery, someone special promised to dance with you. Unfortunately, you couldn't be at Emma's wedding and so tonight, Harry, would you give Sue the honour of dancing with her, please?

It just remains for me to say, that I hope you all enjoy the rest of the evening with Bob & Sue and their wonderful family in celebration.

Thank You.

Testimonies

Julie's Testimony (Bob's Sister)

Robert's Stroke:

Monday morning, I visited my mum. She had fallen over the previous day and broken her arm. I had given her some bigger clothes as I thought these would fit over her cast better. We had just finished lunch and I was about to leave when my parents received a call from Sue. She told us Robert had collapsed at work and was currently in hospital with a suspected stroke. This came as a shock, but he had suffered from fatigue for a while, although to have collapsed was unexpected. There was nothing we could do at that time, so I went home and awaited news.

It was all going well as we were told my brother should be out of hospital within a few days. Hearing this news, I felt calm. On Friday, Mitch and I went to see Robert in hospital. I have to say he didn't look as well as I thought and was quite disoriented. I was also surprised to see Sue, as I thought she was visiting him in the afternoon. But Robert had texted Sue to say he'd moved wards overnight, so Sue decided to come in early to help settle him in.

Sue explained her concerns as she noticed my brother's deterioration. I remember Sue was brilliant in getting Robert help.

She told the nurses that something was very wrong and asked them to page the doctor. When the doctor arrived, Sue asked if my brother could have another scan as she knew something wasn't right. Even though Robert had undergone a previous scan, this only showed a minor stroke which he had received treatment for. The doctor could see a rapid deterioration so organised for another scan to be done urgently. This is something I will always be grateful to Sue and the doctor for, it undoubtedly saved Robert's life. I don't think I would have been so confident to ask.

By that evening, Mitch and I were back at the hospital as my brother had been put into a coma and was being blue lighted to Romford. When I saw him, I couldn't believe how much worse he looked from the morning. I was still feeling positive, though, and it really helped to have all the family around me. The first operation didn't work so Robert had to have another one. I knew it was serious but have only just realised how little his chances of survival were!

A few days passed but my brother remained in a coma. I remember being with my parents as they received a call from Sue to say the medic had said Robert's brainstem was affected, and he wasn't going to make it. I couldn't believe it, I always thought he would survive. We all rushed to the hospital. It was very emotional, we were all upset. I remember ringing my friends, who know Robert well, telling them he was not going to survive.

The next few days were a blur. I describe it as easily the worst week of my life. I didn't want to be an only child, and this upset me. Mitch kept driving us up to Romford so we could see my brother as much as possible.

I remember on one occasion, Robert was coughing slightly, which was the first time I'd heard it. Mitch said to me, "I don't think he is going to die as he was coughing yesterday." I dismissed this because the doctors had told us all he was brainstem dead, and they had done tests. Little did I know what would happen!

On the day life support was being switched off, I decided I wanted to be with my parents. I remember seeing a rainbow as we drove across the Strood. It wasn't long before we were nearly at their house when my phone started to ring, but I didn't pick it up as I knew it would be the call to say my brother had passed away or so I thought.

As soon as I pulled onto my parents' driveway, they appeared at the front door and came over to the car to tell me Robert had opened his eyes and was coming out of the coma. I couldn't believe it. I was happy but very cautious as I was worried how bad and what his quality of life would be. We all wanted to see Robert and made our way to the hospital. We could see he had a very long recovery journey ahead, but at least there was hope.

Once his friends and family learnt of this miracle, a lot of people wanted to visit to help him recover. Sue asked me to organise a visiting rota as my brother was only allowed two visitors at a time and I didn't want people travelling to Romford and then not able to see him. I also wanted my brother to have at least one visitor a day as I thought that would aid his recovery. I am proud to say he had so many friends that this was achieved.

It was hard visiting my brother. As he couldn't speak, it was a one-way conversation. I used to think of things I was going to tell him before I went. I know Dad used to tell him the football scores. I was very pleased when Robert's tracheotomy was removed. I thought it was a big leap forward. I remember when he tried to speak but I couldn't understand him. A nurse told him, "Don't worry your voice will come back," and it did, she was right.

When my brother was at Northwick hospital it was a long way to travel. I didn't like him being so far away but knew it was good for his recovery. Apart from Sue, we were one of the last people to visit him there. Covid was getting worse and there was talk of a lockdown.

I remember taking Robert to the hospital shops and restaurants for a change of scenery. I have this lovely photo of us both having a sandwich. I've shown this to a lot of people who couldn't believe how far he had come and how much better he looked.

Sue worked so hard to get the house ready for my brother to be able to come home before lockdown. It was a big relief when I learnt he had arrived safely. He must have been so happy to finally be in his own home and with only days to spare.

It doesn't bear thinking about what his life would have been like if Sue hadn't got him home as he would have been stuck in his ward with no rehabilitation and no visitors. Sue, Emma, and Will worked so hard making sure he did his exercises. I believe he improved more than if he had stayed at hospital even without Covid.

I would also like to give credit to Robert. I never saw him depressed or moaning about how his stroke affected him. He seemed to take it in his stride and worked hard to give himself the best recovery possible. The NHS staff could also see this and were happy to give him more help as he achieved results.

I will always be grateful to Sue; she has been a wonderful caring wife and certainly encouraged him along the way. It is lovely to see them so happy together especially playing with Imogen their first Grandchild and now Milo too.

I asked Robert one day if he saw a bright tunnel when he was in a coma as it is often recorded that this is what happens. He told me that he has no memory whatsoever of being at Romford and no tunnels. I told him I was surprised he didn't remember as I visited him almost every single day!!! Lol

Cheryl's Testimony (Sue's Sister)

My recollection of the day I heard Bob was poorly.

I remember Sue calling me to say Bob became unwell at work and may have had a mild stroke. He was taken to Colchester General Hospital; I couldn't believe it. Bob did have some previous health issues with fatigue and used to become exhausted if he did too much in one day but to learn that he had had a stroke really surprised me. Sue kept me informed that day he was admitted to hospital, and we were led to believe he was doing very well and would be home quickly.

On the Friday, we thought maybe he would be coming home for the weekend as he had been talking and was cheery. I remember Sue called me and I was expecting her to say that Bob would be going home. However, it was the call that made my heart sink. "Cheryl," she said, "Bob has taken a turn for the worse, please get hold of my kids and tell them to come to the hospital urgently. Bob is critical, they are preparing him for brain surgery, and we are waiting to see if a specialist hospital can take him, Colchester can't do that here." In a panicked voice I heard, "Just get my kids here I can't leave Bob, Cheryl, its critical!"

As I sat at my place of work I remember thinking 'How can this be?' I knew I had to help Sue get the message to her kids and to the hospital, so I just told the office to tell my manager that I had to go, and explained my sister had called me and that her husband was very poorly and might not make it and then I just left.

Once in my car, I phoned Emma and told her I was coming to get her. She is a hairdresser and was worried about how she would leave her client. Silly little things like that popped into to our heads but we had to get to Bob. I then managed to inform Jim and Mike who were also on their way. It seemed like a blur, but we all managed to get to the hospital. When we arrived, I saw my brother-in-law in a coma, the tubes and life support and medical equipment were keeping him as stable as possible.

We then travelled to Romford Queen's Hospital. The ambulance left, and we all followed. On arriving at Queen's, we learnt Bob had survived the journey and was going to be prepared for surgery. We saw him briefly with the ambulance crew before he was taken into critical care and again for a brief moment, once he'd returned from surgery. When we left the hospital it was very late.

However, Bob needed another emergency operation to relieve more pressure on his brain. It felt like we were all in a living nightmare as Bob was not waking up and he should have by then. I felt out of control, very emotional, but had to try to stay strong and positive. As hours went by, Bob was still not responding, and those hours started to turn into days.

The family were told different things about Bob's condition and there seemed to be a difference of opinion on his outlook or chance of recovery and lack of response. The family had tough decisions to make when they were told it was very unlikely Bob would wake up from the coma due to damage to the brain stem. I kept thinking how could this happen to such a lovely man.

I remember going outside and having words with the great man in the sky, blaming him, saying it was not fair, and that he needed to rethink how he makes these things happen as I wouldn't be trusting him again! I went back in and told Sue I had a word with God, and I was very cross with him for putting Bob and the family through this. Sue told me to get back out there and tell him you're sorry and that you do trust him, you are just angry, God is not to blame. I did of course say sorry.

There were lots of tears, worry, and anxiety for us all in those traumatic days. My sister Sue was very strong and although she found it hard to see Bob so poorly, despite the decisions she and her children were going to have to make, Sue was a rock for Bob and her family.

Then came the day we were going to say goodbye to our dear Bob. It had been delayed by a day as some tests on Bob's heart had not taken place. I remembered thinking those recipients to the transplants were probably being prepped to receive Bob's organs and someone was going to receive his heart.

This day was going to be difficult enough for my sister and her children, so Rab and I offered to drive the family to the hospital if they wanted us to. I remember Charlie said he was going to drive Mike. Sue, Emma and Will travelled with me, while Rab drove Jim and Lauren.

As we left the bungalow, a beautiful rainbow appeared above it. All of us saw it and when I turned on my car ignition, the angels song by Robbie Williams started playing on the radio. I also noticed that the rainbow seemed to follow us as we joined the A12. Sue said it was a sign. I knew she was thinking that God was going to look after Bob. Sue called the convoy behind us, and they all heard the song.

Just as we were about twenty minutes from the hospital, Sue received a call from Queen's hospital asking if we had left yet. Sue told them we were twenty minutes away. When they said they would wait until we got there, Sue said No, tell me now. They said they thought Bob was trying to open his eyes and that the transplant procedure was on hold.

We were so pleased, happy, and elated, but could not believe what we had just heard. I remember walking in behind Sue. The kids stood on one side of their dad's bed with Sue and a doctor was on the other side. As Sue called Bob's name, he immediately opened those big blue eyes and then his eyes moved to look in the direction of Sue's voice. None of us could believe it. Everyone was so happy! 'It's a miracle,' we thought. But that was just the beginning.

Sue never gave up on her husband, always believing he would walk again. She had been fighting so hard for Bob to the point where she needed to take time out to safeguard her own mental health and wellbeing. I know she found it hard not to visit Bob for a couple of days, but she needed her own space and time to heal from the trauma she had experienced. I would visit her at home along with close friends and talk things through. Her kids were also very supportive to their Mum and Dad and were there for them both.

On the days when Bob came home you could see how much Sue really cared, her unconditional love for Bob was so clear for all to see. Sue was a great advocate from both his time in hospital, liaising with doctors and consultants about any changes to his condition, to providing twenty-four hour care at home. Sue was so determined to help Bob become mobile again, she never gave up working with Bob, always encouraging him to complete his physio on a daily basis.

In time he learnt to build his body back up towards independence again, lockdown and lots of physio, stimulation exercises, tears, sweat and hard work, were all a part of the process into giving Bob the best opportunity in his recovery. Obviously, Bob had to fight hard. As his strength began to return, he started walking with a frame and then progressed to a walking stick, he is returning to his old hobbies and has regained a good quality of life. He has his mobility scooter which helps him to access and enjoy the wider community which he loves. Skip to the now...... Bob you are a Miracle!

BOB, TOP MAN, TOP BROTHER-IN- LAW..................BOB IS BACK.

I can't thank you enough for all the support and advice that you have given me over the recent couple of years since your recovery. What would we have all done without you?

I am so pleased that we all have a chance to continue sharing good times together from wonderful family events to holidays with you and Sue and of course your lovely BBQs.

My sister Sue, you are a very loyal, kind, caring, loving and thoughtful person. You are always there to help and support those in need, especially family and friends close to you. Anyone who is fortunate enough to have you in their life is truly blessed. I am so lucky to have you as my sister and best friend!.

John and Daphne's Testimony (Bob's Parents)

Memories of Robert's Stroke:

We will refer to our son as we have always done, as Robert.

Monday 11th November did not start well. Daphne had fallen on a walk the previous day and had broken her arm in two places. It seemed strange that Robert had not phoned to see how she was. Then Sue rang us, and the day became much worse. Our son had collapsed at work and had been taken to hospital, but Sue had been told that they thought he would be home in two to three days.

However, Robert's condition deteriorated, and we received a call to come to the hospital as soon as possible. It was distressing to see our son in the hospital bed motionless as he had been placed in a coma to prepare for surgery at Romford.

The days after the operations became very painful for the entire family, and the decision to start to remove Robert's life support on the Friday seemed to be the end. Sue had said that all the family could be with Robert in the final stages, but we decided to say goodbye to our son on Thursday afternoon.

On the Friday, we received a call to say that while Sue and the children were on their way to the hospital to say goodbye to Robert, Sue had received a call and was told that they could not go ahead with turning off life support and organ donation as they thought Robert was responding with his eyes. Sue said that they were at the hospital and Robert had opened his eyes when she called his name. This was truly amazing news.

Over the next few weeks, our son made progress each time we visited him, and we were so pleased when after Christmas he was repatriated back to Colchester. When visiting Robert, we were able to sit in on some of the therapy sessions (who needs a song sheet for We'll Meet Again).

The improvement in our son's recovery was plain to see. The care and attention that he received at all three hospitals has been exceptional and was a credit to the much-maligned Health Service, well done to you all.

The final move in his recovery was to Northwick Park, which was going well until Covid hit the ward and it was felt that it would be safer to get Robert home. After an inspection of his bungalow, he was able to stay at home to continue his improvement.

Once Covid rules and restrictions had subsided, it was so nice to be able to see our son and observe his progress, always supervised by our kind and caring daughter-in-law, Sue.

We were so delighted when Robert returned to Colchester Golf Club and started the long process of playing again. The club and the marvelous members and his club team The Coconuts have been so supportive in making sure that he is welcome.

We must acknowledge four events that have lifted the whole family, the wedding of Emma and Will and also Jim and Lauren, plus the birth of our great granddaughter Imogen and our newly born great grandson Milo, all bring smiles to all our faces.

When our son came out of the coma, it was clear that he would be unable to return to work as he had a long road ahead of him with rehabilitation, so a board meeting was set up for myself, Jim, and Mike to meet with Robert's fellow directors to discuss options, where we agreed various matters, and eventually he sold his shares back to the company, which meant that he had the financial means to retire early.

Finally, we would like to say how proud we are of our entire family who have been so supportive.

Of our daughter, Julie and her husband Mitch who have always been available to help out when asked. Julie organised visiting rotas and Mitch drove to various hospitals.

Of our grandchildren and their partners who have always been there to give support to their parents and each other. Always lending a helping hand with different tasks throughout what were difficult times for all, yet still always supporting your Mum and Dad. Well done, Jim, Mike, Emma, Lauren, Charlie and Will.

Of our daughter-in-law, Sue, who spent a lot of time supporting, watching, and encouraging our son to complete his physio exercises and rehab at all three hospitals and could therefore take this knowledge home with her. With knowledge of the medical issues concerning brain injury and the effects of a stroke, she often consulted with the medical staff to ensure Robert received the best possible care and to gain valuable insight into the best way to help our son achieve the desired outcome and rehabilitation. Sue has been outstandingly brilliant as she has taken the lead in Robert's recovery in both hospital and at home, particularly during lockdown.

And of our son Robert who, from the moment he opened his eyes, has been so positive in his attitude. Learning to walk again, talk again, and not being afraid to explore the use of equipment to help him regain a good quality of life.

We look forward to our son continuing to make progress in the future, and we thank you all for the help, care and attention that has been given to him. The support Robert has received from work colleagues, family, and friends, at home and at the hospital visits were so much a big part of his recovery.

God bless you all.

Sue's Testimony

My testimony is this book itself and I am so grateful to everyone who played a vital part in Bob's miraculous journey and recovery. Thank you too for helping me to tell the story.

My wish is that this book brings hope and inspiration to help others who may find themselves in a similar situation. I hope it encourages you to never give up!

I also hope that one day, Dr El-rekaby can have the Stroke Service he dreams of.......

'A Stroke Service where all care runs in one place, for patients to be able to receive treatment and admission to ITU if required, without the need to transfer to another hospital for lifesaving brain surgery. To have access to intensive rehabilitation within the same department. To have a centre that would provide everything from beginning to end and closer to the patients home.'

I wish too that everyone could have a collective like 'Team Bob' in their time of need!

Who knows, maybe Bob's miracle will be worthy of a film or TV series to reach even more people and, with the profits made from such a dream, we may just achieve this!
Believe in Miracles!

May you see the joy of many rainbows.

Bob's Testimony

My Stroke Journey:

My recollection of events is sporadic and somewhat varied. I remember on that fateful day in November, whilst in my office, my left leg started shaking uncontrollably. I called for help from my colleagues and, with their assistance, I got down to the floor, which is the safest place given the circumstances.

They telephoned Sue and she came straight to the office with my daughter Emma and arrived just before the paramedics. There were three paramedics, I recall one of them was training. They asked me lots of questions, and then took me into the ambulance as I needed to go to hospital, Emma accompanied me, with Sue following us in the car.

I can remember the journey and the trainee medic being asked if sirens were needed, she said yes and then we raced to the hospital. I recall looking at Emma as the journey was fast. I have no recollection of anything else until around Christmas time, except some things in Romford but I have no idea what really happened.

I remember trying to communicate with Sue in Romford using my eyes and then we moved on to an alphabet chart. On Christmas Day the family all came over to see me and I remember we gave out the Secret Santa presents which had been organised a few weeks before my stroke had occurred. I'd brought Will a joke present and can recall Sue asking me if I remembered, which I did.

As I was bedbound, I hadn't seen a mirror for weeks, even though I'm pretty much bald, I was told the hair I had was spiky and just stood upright. Emma, being a hairdresser, arrived one day and used the clippers to cut it. I was amazed as the hair fell; it was so long!

In January 2020, I was transferred to Colchester but have no memory of this, in fact, many things I remember from early on, didn't actually happen and those that did, I can't remember!

At Colchester I had so many family and friends wanting to visit me, my sister, Julie, did a rota. Sue arranged for many friends to massage my hands and feet, to keep my senses working, I enjoyed this, I think I got more than one massage on the same day as every time someone offered, I always said yes. People used to laugh at this.

Sue, the children and my parents visited every day, which I enjoyed. The hospital arranged daily activities like physio, speech therapy and singing groups. I was still confined to bed, unable to walk and only fed by a feeding tube. One day Sue brought our dogs, Archie & Honey, to see me. I heard them before I saw them, it was great even though Archie accidentally sat on my feeding tube and pulled it out.

I can remember Sue had printed out pictures of us, our family, and dogs and these were pinned to the board next to my bed, which was great and a good talking point. Lots of people visited me, normally for only a short time, as I got tired quickly. Some patients had no visitors, which was a negative for their recovery.

After a few assessments, I was transferred to Northwick Hospital for intensive rehab. This hospital was near Harrow in Middlesex which was a long way to visit but I appreciated it would be good for my recovery. I had just come off the feeding tube and solids were gradually being introduced. Sue was allowed to feed me a cup of tea by spoon.

Northwick was large and somewhat dated, but they installed a daily timetable for me, to include physio and speech therapy and every day was planned, with visiting also planned around this. I appreciated visiting was more difficult because of the distance, but I looked forward to seeing people. Sometimes family and friends would take me in my wheelchair to the shops on the ground floor and buy prawn sandwiches from the on-site M&S. This was a lovely treat away from hospital food.

I remember the first day I was allowed to clean my teeth at the sink, which sounds quite basic but for me then was a welcome novelty. I slowly progressed to short walks with a frame and getting out of bed with assistance. My speech was improving, which was very important to me as one of my goals was to do my father of the bride speech at Emma and Will's wedding. My recovery was remarkable with plenty of hard work from all sides.

With Covid breaking, they discussed my return home with me, but needed to arrange equipment from the local council. Because of Covid, we knew this would be impossible to get in time, so Sue went to the local mobility shop and purchased it all. She sent me photos, and I was able to show the O.T. and they agreed I was able to go home, subject to them doing a home visit. Two days later I was in a volunteer car with two OTs on my way home. The next day we learnt that the hospital was in Covid lockdown.

My time at home was another turning point. Our daughter, Emma, and her finance Will had moved in to help Sue (hospital had insisted on this). They looked after the house and home, and Sue concentrated solely on looking after me and helping me with physio.

Because of the Covid Pandemic and the negative impact it had within the NHS, the referral had been lost in the system, which meant I had no home community physio visits to start with, so Sue researched the internet to look up exercises and used her knowledge gained when previously visiting me in physio sessions in hospital.

We started with basic exercises until I mastered them and progressed up. We found my brain soon learnt, and it was only a matter of days before I progressed to the next level.

We worked on balance and walking, plus coordination and speech. I wouldn't have achieved so much if we hadn't done all this. When Covid restrictions were relaxed, and things were safer, we began receiving many visits from family and friends, which was great.

I had progressed from wheelchair to walking frame and then to a walking stick. There were many moments along the way, where we learnt to laugh, like when I would lose my balance or wobble a bit and sometimes spill or break things. I remember getting out of bed one morning thinking I'll make Sue a cup of tea, (something I'd done for 30 years but not recently), I sat on the bed to get changed and just fell off! A bit of advice for anyone who is unfortunate to be in a similar situation, it does help if you learn to laugh. Another time I attempted to make a cup of tea and managed to knock over a whole mug all down the kitchen cupboards and all over the floor, Sue calmly came over and cleared it up. We just laughed.

My recovery was helped by our dogs as well, especially Honey. She's a lab/retriever cross and has taken it upon herself to be my assistance dog. To this day she watches my every move and is always there if I fall or lose balance. If I try and do exercises on the floor, we have to put her in another room as she thinks I've fallen over and comes to my rescue.

In the days after coming home, I would have my usual evening bath and Sue would help me in and out of it to keep me safe. Once I'd finished, Sue helped me with my dressing gown. I would often feel quite tired at the end of the day and needed a bit of extra help with the walking frame, so Sue would help me to bed. One day the routine changed as it was a bit later than normal, I decided I'd have my bath the following morning.

As usual, Sue helped me to get out of the bath safely and once I was dressed, she gave me my frame and then she went to the kitchen to wash up the breakfast things. I felt ok using the frame and began to walk into the hallway on my own. Honey saw I was approaching. She knew this was not the normal routine, so barked loudly at Sue as if to say, "What are you doing? You normally help!"

We have learnt to never give up hope, we laugh at mishaps, and both family and friends are very important, but we always knew this. With hard work by patient and carer most things can be overcome - and don't be afraid to use as many aids as you need. My best buy is my mobility scooter, which gives me independence and freedom.

I like to remain positive and, as Sue would say, every cloud has a silver lining. Although not planned, my stroke enabled me to retire early and enjoy life without the hassle and stress of work, something that I don't miss!

One of my main goals was to walk my lovely daughter Emma down the aisle and dance with her on her wedding day. I achieved both of these and the father of the bride's speech too. A great highlight in my life.

Another strange highlight was walking on a beach and paddling in the sea with help from Sue in Majorca in 2023, as we were able to travel with the help of airport special assistance. For some this may seem like a mundane activity but to me it was so surreal.

I am also back to playing golf which I absolutely love, and, with the support of my friends at the club and my old work colleague Kevin, I am able to enjoy this hobby once again.

Sue has read the manuscript of this book to me, and I am amazed how all my family and friends got together to help my recovery. It is truly outstanding, and I thank you all. I'd especially like to pay tribute to my great friend, Clive, who sadly passed away in Thailand on September 2023 age 70. In the days to follow after my homecoming, we would regularly facetime and catch up with each other. He always brought a smile to people's faces and was always so encouraging of my recovery. RIP Clive; sorely missed but never forgotten.

On this note, I'd also like to pay tribute to Rechel Erenia who was an exceptional nurse and a kind and caring young man lost to us too soon. R.I.P 12th June 2023

Above all, I would like to acknowledge that my recovery was only possible because of Sue's dedication and willingness to accept a change in her husband and the fact that we both worked together as a team, overcoming obstacles, and remaining positive throughout. Thank you, Sue, I love you so much! x

Medical Terms and Procedures Explained

MRI Scan

$\mathbf{M}$agnetic resonance imaging (MRI) is a medical imaging technique used in radiology to form pictures of the anatomy and the physiological processes inside the body. MRI scanners use strong magnetic fields, magnetic field gradients, and radio waves to generate images of the organs in the body. MRI does not involve X-rays or the use of ionizing radiation, which distinguishes it from computed tomography (CT) and positron emission tomography (PET) scans. MRI is a medical application of nuclear magnetic resonance (NMR) which can also be used for imaging in other NMR applications, such as NMR spectroscopy.

MRI is widely used in hospitals and clinics for medical diagnosis, staging and follow-up of disease. Compared to CT, MRI provides better contrast in images of soft tissues, e.g., in the brain or abdomen. However, it may be perceived as less comfortable by patients, due to the usually longer and louder measurements with the subject in a long, confining tube, although "open" MRI designs mostly relieve this. Additionally, implants and other non-removable metal in the body can pose a risk and may exclude some patients from undergoing an MRI examination safely. *(1)*

(1) Wikipedia contributors. (2024, April 16). Magnetic resonance imaging. In Wikipedia, The Free Encyclopedia. Retrieved 17:11, May 8, 2024, from https://en.wikipedia.org/w/index. php?title=Magnetic_resonance_imaging&oldid=1219184259

CT Scan

A computed tomography scan (CT scan; formerly called computed axial tomography scan or CAT scan) is a medical imaging technique used to obtain detailed internal images of the body. The personnel that perform CT scans are called radiographers or radiology technologists.

CT scanners use a rotating X-ray tube and a row of detectors placed in a gantry to measure X-ray attenuations by different tissues inside the body. The multiple X-ray measurements taken from different angles are then processed on a computer using tomographic reconstruction algorithms to produce tomographic (cross-sectional) images (virtual "slices") of a body. CT scans can be used in patients with metallic implants or pacemakers, for whom magnetic resonance imaging (MRI) is contraindicated. *(1)*

(1) Wikipedia contributors. (2024, May 2). CT scan. In Wikipedia, The Free Encyclopedia. Retrieved 17:22, May 8, 2024, from https://en.wikipedia.org/w/index.php?title=CT_ scan&oldid=1221924588

A Vertebral Artery Dissection (VAD)

A flap-like tear of the inner lining of the vertebral artery, which is located in the neck and supplies blood to the brain. After the tear, blood enters the arterial wall and forms a blood clot, thickening the artery wall and often impeding blood flow. The symptoms of vertebral artery dissection include head and neck pain and intermittent or permanent stroke symptoms such as difficulty speaking, impaired coordination, and visual loss. It is usually diagnosed with a contrast-enhanced CT or MRI scan. *(1)*

(1) Wikipedia contributors. (2024, January 6). Vertebral artery dissection. In Wikipedia, The Free Encyclopedia. Retrieved 14:49, May 8, 2024, from https://en.wikipedia.org/w/index. php?title=Vertebral_artery_dissection&oldid=1194030683

Hydrocephalus

Hydrocephalus is a condition in which an accumulation of cerebrospinal fluid (CSF) occurs within the brain.[1] This typically causes increased pressure inside the skull. Older people may have headaches, double vision, poor balance, urinary incontinence, personality changes, or mental impairment. *(1)*

(1) Wikipedia contributors. (2024, April 30). Hydrocephalus. In Wikipedia, The Free Encyclopedia. Retrieved 15:45, May 8, 2024, from https://en.wikipedia.org/w/index. php?title=Hydrocephalus&oldid=1221570882

A Cerebellar Infarct or Cerebellar Stroke

Cerebellar strokes account for only 2-3% of the 600,000 strokes that occur each year in the United States. They are far less common than strokes which occur in the cerebral hemispheres. In recent years mortality rates have decreased due to advancements in health care which include earlier diagnosis through MRI and CT scanning. Advancements have also been made which allow earlier management for common complications of cerebellar stroke such as brainstem compression and hydrocephalus. Research is still needed in the area of cerebellar stroke management; however, several factors may lead to poor outcomes in individuals who have a cerebellar stroke. These factors include:

- Declining levels of consciousness
- New signs of brainstem involvement
- Progressing Hydrocephalus
- Stroke to the midline of the cerebellum (a.k.a. the vermis). *(1)*

(1) Wikipedia contributors. (2023, December 9). Cerebellar

stroke syndrome. In Wikipedia, The Free Encyclopedia. Retrieved 18:04, May 8, 2024, from https://en.wikipedia.org/w/index. php?title=Cerebellar_stroke_syndrome&oldid=1188996449

Tracheostomy

Tracheotomy (/ˌtreɪkiˈɒtəmi/, UK also /ˌtræki-/), or tracheostomy, is a surgical airway management procedure which consists of making an incision (cut) on the anterior aspect (front) of the neck and opening a direct airway through an incision in the trachea (windpipe). The resulting stoma (hole) can serve independently as an airway or as a site for a tracheal tube or tracheostomy tube to be inserted; this tube allows a person to breathe without the use of the nose or mouth. There are 4 main reasons why someone would receive a tracheotomy:

Emergency airway access

- Airway access for prolonged mechanical ventilation
- Functional or mechanical upper airway obstruction
- Decreased/incompetent clearance of tracheobronchial secretions. *(1)*

(1) Wikipedia contributors. (2024, April 9). Tracheotomy. In Wikipedia, The Free Encyclopedia. Retrieved 17:54, May 8, 2024, from https://en.wikipedia.org/w/index. php?title=Tracheotomy&oldid=1218118398

External Ventricular Drain

An external ventricular drain (EVD), also known as a ventriculostomy or extra ventricular drain, is a device used in neurosurgery to treat hydrocephalus and relieve elevated intracranial pressure when the normal flow of cerebrospinal fluid (CSF) inside the brain is obstructed. An EVD is a flexible plastic catheter placed by a neurosurgeon or neurointensivist and managed by intensive care unit (ICU) physicians and nurses. The purpose of external ventricular drainage is to divert fluid from the ventricles of the brain and allow for monitoring of intracranial pressure. An EVD must be placed in a center with full neurosurgical capabilities, because immediate neurosurgical intervention can be needed if a complication of EVD placement, such as bleeding, is encountered. (1)

(1) Wikipedia contributors. (2023, December 3). External ventricular drain. In Wikipedia, The Free Encyclopedia. Retrieved 17:25, May 8, 2024, from https://en.wikipedia.org/w/index. php?title=External_ventricular_drain&oldid=1188063303

Craniectomy (Posterior Fossa Decompression)

Decompressive craniectomy (crani- + -ectomy) is a neurosurgical procedure in which part of the skull is removed to allow a swelling or herniating brain room to expand without being squeezed. It is performed on victims of traumatic brain injury, stroke, Chiari malformation, and other conditions associated with raised intracranial pressure. Use of this surgery is controversial.

Though the procedure is considered a last resort, some evidence suggests that it does improve outcomes by lowering intracranial pressure (ICP), the pressure within the skull. Raised intracranial pressure is very often debilitating or fatal because it causes compression of the brain and restricts cerebral blood flow. The aim of decompressive craniectomy is to reduce this pressure. The part of the skull that is removed is called a bone flap. A study has shown that the larger the removed bone flap is, the more ICP is reduced. *(1)*

(1) Wikipedia contributors. (2023, December 30). Decompressive craniectomy. In Wikipedia, The Free Encyclopedia. Retrieved 17:39, May 8, 2024, from https://en.wikipedia.org/w/index. php?title=Decompressive_craniectomy&oldid=1192593492

Bibliography

(1) *YouTube. (2009, July 18). It's going to be alright by Sarah Groves.*
     Retrieved 10:30, May 11, 2024,
     from It's Going to Be All Right - Sara Groves (youtube.com)
     Spark People.

(2) *Wikipedia contributors. (2024, April 16). Magnetic resonance*
     imaging. In Wikipedia, The Free Encyclopedia. Retrieved
     17:11, May 8, 2024, from https://en.wikipedia.org/w/index.
     php?title=Magnetic_resonance_imaging&oldid=1219184259

(3) *Wikipedia contributors. (2024, May 2). CT scan.*
     In Wikipedia, The Free Encyclopedia. Retrieved 17:22,
     May 8, 2024, from https://en.wikipedia.org/w/index.
     php?title=CT_scan&oldid=1221924588

(4) *Wikipedia contributors. (2024, January 6). Vertebral artery*
     dissection. In Wikipedia, The Free Encyclopedia. Retrieved
     14:49, May 8, 2024, from https://en.wikipedia.org/w/index.
     php?title=Vertebral_artery_dissection&oldid=1194030683

(5) *Wikipedia contributors. (2024, April 30). Hydrocephalus.*
     In Wikipedia, The Free Encyclopedia. Retrieved 15:45,
     May 8, 2024, from https://en.wikipedia.org/w/index.
     php?title=Hydrocephalus&oldid=1221570882

(6) *Wikipedia contributors. (2023, December 9). Cerebellar stroke*
     syndrome. In Wikipedia, The Free Encyclopedia. Retrieved
     18:04, May 8, 2024, from https://en.wikipedia.org/w/index.
     php?title=Cerebellar_stroke_syndrome&oldid=1188996449

(7) *Wikipedia contributors. (2024, April 9). Tracheotomy.*
     In Wikipedia, The Free Encyclopedia. Retrieved 17:54,
     May 8, 2024, from https://en.wikipedia.org/w/index.
     php?title=Tracheotomy&oldid=1218118398

(8) *Wikipedia contributors. (2023, December 3). External*
     ventricular drain. In Wikipedia, The Free Encyclopedia.
     Retrieved 17:25, May 8, 2024, from https://en.wikipedia.org/w/
     index.php?title=External_ventricular_drain&oldid=1188063303

(9) *Wikipedia contributors. (2023, December 30). Decompressive*
     craniectomy. In Wikipedia, The Free Encyclopedia. Retrieved
     17:39, May 8, 2024, from https://en.wikipedia.org/w/index.
     php?title=Decompressive_craniectomy&oldid=1192593492

Acknowledgments

Medical Teams

To the remarkable Consultants, Specialist, Doctors, Surgeons, Nurses, Occupational Therapists, Physio Therapists, Speech Therapists, Community Teams, and all staff who looked after Bob at Colchester General Hospital Stroke Unit, the Queens Hospital Neuro ITU Romford, and the Northwick Park Hospital Intense Physio Rehabilitation Unit Harrow. We owe Bob's life to you and words cannot express our sincere gratitude. Your skill and commitment to preserve life and to enable miracles like this to happen, leaves us all speechless and full of admiration. *Thank you* x

To My Children and Their Partners

I would like to thank my children, Jim, Mike, and Emma for all your love, strength, loyalty, and supporting me and your dad throughout this whole incredible journey. To your partners, Lauren, Charlie and Will, thank you for all you did, not only to support your partners, but also for being there for myself and Bob. You have all shown the true meaning of what a family is all about. We shared the pain, the tears, the sadness, the laughter and the joy and the many different signs along the way. With everything you have collectively done for me and your dad, I cannot tell you enough how proud I am of you all. *I love you x*

To Bob's Parents

John and Daphne, I couldn't wish for a better mother-in-law and father-in-law. As parents, to see your son so close to leaving you and watching him and your daughter-in-law and grandchildren go through so much is unimaginable. Thank you both for all the support and love given to me and my children and for ensuring that Emma and Will's wedding went ahead! *Thank you, Love Sue x*

To My Sister Cheryl

You are the true definition of what a sister is and should be. You are not only my sister, but you are also my very best friend, and one in whom I can trust. You never let me down and are always there for me, through thick and thin, good or bad, rain or shine. Thank you for walking beside me and dancing with me through life, whether the song that's playing is happy or sad. *'Life isn't about waiting for the storm to pass...its learning to dance in the rain'* and knowing that when the sun comes out to shine, a rainbow will hopefully appear! *I love you, Sis! x*

Family and Their Extended Families

Thank you for all your support and the many visits to Bob in all three hospitals and for walking beside the Bloomfield family throughout this journey. Special thanks to Bob's sister Julie for coordinating the 'Team Bob' visiting rota and for helping to support your brother. I would especially like to thank you all for the love and care shown to me, my children, their partners, and Bob's parents at such a traumatic time. *Thank you, Love Sue x*

Special Friends

To our closest and very special friends. Thank you for being there in the darkest of times, helping to pull Bob through. Thank you for also being there for me, checking I was ok, inviting me to eat at your table and staying with me to eat at mine, going for walks with the dogs, wiping away my tears and seeing me at my very lowest ebb, but still loving me. All of you have shown the true meaning of what friendship is all about; a true friend is with you in the good times and stays by your side in the bad times. To all of you, old and new, who are always there in both the Yin and Yang of life, who remain here dancing to each song as the journey continues, thank you for partying with us and helping us to celebrate the miracle of Bob! *Love you all and thank you x*

TAG Family

To my PACK! I didn't know when we met all those years ago how our friendships would grow. But I will always be grateful that our love of dogs and dog agility led me to such a kind, loving, and loyal circle of friends. They say that a man's best friend is his dog, so how lucky was I that Archie and Honey led me to such special people: my 'TAG Family.' Thank you for being there! *I love you all x*

Archie And Honey

Our loyal and faithful dogs. Thank you for your unconditional love, affectionate cuddles, and sensitive caring natures. I guess fate played its part and you were meant to find your forever home with us! Both being rescue dogs, you actually defined the meaning of 'rescue' more than anyone will ever know! *I love you x*

Imogen (Immy) Our Beautiful Granddaughter and Milo Our Beautiful Grandson

Immy, you were a major part of this journey, even before you were born! You are the kindest and most caring of souls and you shine from within.

And Milo, the newest member of Team Bob to date. Another reason for your grandad to keep thriving and I can see already that you too are a beautiful soul.

We can't wait to create more special moments with you both. *Nana and Grandad Bob love you both so very much x*

Bob
Thank you for being such a lovely and kind caring man and a wonderful husband to me, dad to our children and grandad to our grandchildren. Your sheer strength and determination to strive forward and to never give up is incredible. I will always be so proud of you. *I love you x*

Remembering all those reading from the heavens:

Mum & Dad
The best parents I could have had. You made me strong. Always in my heart. *Love Sue x*

Clive
A dear friend to Bob. Thank you for all your love and support given to Bob. *Rest in Peace, dear friend x*

Rechel Erenia
An exceptional nurse and a kind and caring young man lost to us too soon. *R.I.P 12th June 2023*

And to the many lives lost during Covid times.
Loved and never forgotten. *xxx*

God
In whom I believe and trust. *Thank you, I love You x*

About the Author

Sue is one of three siblings raised by loving parents. She attended mainstream education before moving on to employment. Sue met Bob when she was nineteen, they married three years later and went on to have three children of their own.

A stay-at-home Mum until the children were of school age, Sue took a new direction, working within the healthcare and charity sectors, where she spent over fifteen years advocating and supporting vulnerable adults.

Spending time with family and friends is especially important to Sue and has always been her main focus. Sue is a person who wears her heart on her sleeve, which is definitely reflected within this book! She loves walking her two dogs and spending time in her garden, surrounded by wildlife and the miracle of nature - including rainbows!

Rainbows have always been signs of hope throughout Sue's life. She has always thought of these as bridges between the physical and spiritual worlds, a divine connection between heaven and earth, a pathway revealing signs of hope and love for anyone open to receiving them.........

Believe in Miracles!

May you see the joy of many rainbows

Printed in Great Britain
by Amazon

57769965R00119